Lonely Planet

Pocket
SHANGHAI
TOP SIGHTS • LOCAL LIFE • MADE EASY

D0092398

Christopher Pitts

In This Book

QuickStart Guide

Your keys to understanding the city – we help you decide what to do and how to do it

Need to Know
Tips for a smooth trip

Neighbourhoods
What's where

Explore Shanghai

The best things to see and do, neighbourhood by neighbourhood

Top Sights
Make the most of your visit

Local Life
The insider's city

The Best of Shanghai

The city's highlights in handy lists to help you plan

Best Walks
See the city on foot

Shanghai's Best...
The best experiences

Survival Guide

Tips and tricks for a seamless, hassle-free city experience

Getting Around
Travel like a local

Essential Information
Including where to stay

Our selection of the city's best places to eat, drink and experience:

◉ **Sights**

⊗ **Eating**

🍷 **Drinking**

✪ **Entertainment**

🔒 **Shopping**

These symbols give you the vital information for each listing:

☏	Telephone Numbers	👶	Family-Friendly
⊘	Opening Hours	🐾	Pet-Friendly
P	Parking	🚌	Bus
⊘	Nonsmoking	⛴	Ferry
@	Internet Access	M	Metro
📶	Wi-Fi Access	S	Subway
⚲	Vegetarian Selection	🚋	Tram
📖	English-Language Menu	🚆	Train

Find each listing quickly on maps for each neighbourhood:

Bar Hemingway

16 🍷 Map p233, B2

Legend has it that Hemi self, wielding a machine rate this timber-pan ered bar during showpiece is a en by Papa an town. Dress s.com; Hôtel Rit ; ⊘6.30pm-2a

---

Lonely Planet's Shanghai

Lonely Planet Pocket Guides are designed to get you straight to the heart of the city.

Inside you'll find all the must-see sights, plus tips to make your visit to each one really memorable. We've split the city into easy-to-navigate neighbourhoods and provided clear maps so you'll find your way around with ease. Our expert authors have searched out the best of the city: walks, food, nightlife and shopping, to name a few. Because you want to explore, our 'Local Life' pages will take you to some of the most exciting areas to experience the real Shanghai.

And of course you'll find all the practical tips you need for a smooth trip: itineraries for short visits, how to get around, and how much to tip the guy who serves you a drink at the end of a long day's exploration.

It's your guarantee of a really great experience.

Our Promise

You can trust our travel information because Lonely Planet authors visit the places we write about, each and every edition. We never accept freebies for positive coverage, so you can rely on us to tell it like it is.

QuickStart Guide 7

Explore Shanghai 21

Worth a Trip:

The Best of Shanghai 105

Shanghai's Best Walks

Shanghai's Best...

Survival Guide 131

QuickStart Guide

Welcome to Shanghai

Positively electric, Shanghai is where China's aspirations come to life. A symbol of the country's emerging status, a byword for opportunity and sophistication, the city is all that and more. Whether you're after food, fashion or futuristic skylines, Shanghai's buzzing confidence and nonstop action make for a veritable roller-coaster ride: hang on and have fun.

The Bund (p24), set against Pudong's skyline
PETER ADAMS/GETTY IMAGES ©

Shanghai
Top Sights

The Bund (p24)

Mainland China's most iconic concession-era backdrop, the Bund encapsulates Shanghai with its postcard-perfect good looks. A dazzling curve of bombastic masonry, it leads the way as one of the city's most stylish destinations.

GRANT FAINT/GETTY IMAGES ©

Shanghai Museum (p28)

Shanghai's best museum by a long shot, this must-see is a marvellous tribute to the path of beauty throughout the millennia, from ancient bronzes and transcendent landscapes to gorgeous ceramic masterpieces.

Yuyuan Gardens & Bazaar (p48)

For some, the Old Town's beleaguered charms are one of the most alluring parts of a Shanghai visit. This classical garden is a fitting contrast to the city's future-now mantra.

Qibao (p102)

When you tire of Shanghai's slick, international modernity, head for the quintessentially Chinese landscapes beyond the city centre. Qibao is the closest of the nearby canal towns, a mere half-hour away on the metro.

FENG WEI PHOTOGRAPHY/GETTY IMAGES ©

TAO IMAGES LIMITED/GETTY IMAGES ©

M50 (p86)

Located in a former cotton mill, the industrially chic M50 is the city's main creative hub. Dozens of edgy galleries and occasional events make this an absorbing place to wander.

Tianzifang (p58)

This engaging warren of *shikumen* (stone-gate house) architecture and hip boutiques is the perfect spot for browsing while soaking up the flavours of the ever-elusive traditional Shanghai neighbourhood.

Jade Buddha Temple (p84)

Despite first impressions, the city does have a strong current of religious tradition. It's best observed in this century-old Buddhist temple, which is witness to a continual stream of worshippers throughout the day.

Xintiandi (p60)

A visitor favourite, this prettified strip of traditional Shanghai housing is probably one of the only places in the world where fine dining, designer shopping and communism intersect.

Shanghai Local Life

Insider tips to help you find the real city

Shanghai is much more than the Bund and Xintiandi – to truly experience the city, you need to get under its skin, an experience best had by exploring small lanes, leafy side streets and old alleyways.

East Nanjing Road (p32)

▶ Historic shops
▶ People watching

Once China's most famous shopping street, E Nanjing Rd is perennially thick with eager shoppers, out-of-towners and neon signs illuminating the night. Take a deep breath and plunge in, but shrug off English-speaking girls dragging victims to overpriced cafes.

Backstreets & Alleyways (p50)

▶ Temples
▶ Antique vendors

Explore the Old Town, following twisting alleyways and stopping to contemplate

yellow-walled temples along the way. There are some fantastic spots here to pick up souvenirs, from faux antiques and local knick-knacks to tailor-made clothing.

Concession-Era Architecture (p72)

▶ Famous residences
▶ Cute boutiques

The French Concession's tree-lined lanes are a world away from Shanghai's busy central neighbourhoods. It's all on a very human scale in this part of town, so take the time to browse through the local boutiques and admire the stylistically diverse century-old villas as you go.

Jing'an Architecture (p88)

▶ Lilong architecture
▶ Diverse shops

Away from the commercial buzz of the main drag (W Nanjing Rd), this area is charmingly detailed with pleasant *lilong* (alleys), its character supplied by a profusion of period architecture.

Hongkou (p44)

▶ Local markets
▶ Street-side snacks

This gritty and somewhat rundown neighbourhood is off most tourist itineraries, but certainly worth a visit for its captivating street life. Visit a local food market, a discount clothing bazaar and the unexpectedly appealing Post Museum.

PartyWorld (p67)

Locals playing Chinese chess, Fuxing Park (p64)

Other great places to experience the city like a local:

Yang's Fry Dumplings (p38)

Jesse (p77)

Nanxiang Steamed Bun Restaurant (p38)

Wujiang Road Food Street (p92)

Bai's Restaurant (p77)

No 88 (p78)

PartyWorld (p67)

Yifu Theatre (p42)

KARL JOHAENDGES/GETTY IMAGES ©

GARDEL BERTRAND/GETTY IMAGES ©

Shanghai Day Planner

Day One

One day in Shanghai? Rise with the sun for early-morning riverside views of the **Bund** (p24) as the city stirs from its slumber. Visit landmark buildings such as the Fairmont Peace Hotel and the HSBC building before strolling down **East Nanjing Road** (p32) to People's Sq and the **Shanghai Museum** (p28) or the **Shanghai Urban Planning Exhibition Hall** (p36).

After a local lunch on **Yunnan Road Food Street** (p37), hop on the metro at People's Sq to shuttle east to Pudong. Explore the fun and interactive **Shanghai History Museum** (p99) or contemplate the Bund from the breezy **Riverside Promenade** (p99), and then take a high-speed lift to one of the world's highest observation decks, inside the **Shanghai World Financial Center** (p99), to put the city in perspective.

As evening falls, return to the Bund for dinner. Try **Lost Heaven** (p36) for Yunnanese, **el Willy** (p38) for Spanish or perhaps a simple meal at **Shanghai Grandmother** (p38). Afterwards, head to any of the nearby bars for cocktails or take an evening river **cruise** (p113).

Day Two

Two days? Pre-empt the crowds with an early start at the Old Town's **Yuyuan Gardens** (p48) before poking around for souvenirs along **Old Street** (p51) or at the **Dongtai Road Antique Market** (p55). While you're wandering the alleyways, don't miss the **Chenxiangge Nunnery** (p50) or the delightful neighbourhood around the **Confucius Temple** (p53).

Make your next stop **Xintiandi** (p60) for lunch – think five-star dumplings at **Din Tai Fung** (p64), dim sum at **Crystal Jade** (p65) or molecular creations at **T8** (p67). Don't linger over your meal for too long, however, as you'll need time to visit the **Shikumen Open House Museum** (p61) afterwards. From here, taxi it to **Tianzifang** (p59) for the afternoon, where you can browse start-up boutiques to your heart's content.

Stop by **Kaiba** (p67) for happy hour before heading out for the evening's dinner. The French Concession is absolutely bursting with choices, so do your homework first. Good picks are **Di Shui Dong** (p64), **Cha's** (p65) and **Southern Barbarian** (p65). Afterwards, wind down with a **foot massage** (p121).

Short on time?
We've arranged Shanghai's must-sees into these day-by-day itineraries to make sure you see the very best of the city in the time you have available.

Day Three

☀ It's another early start to the day – absorb the morning's clarity at **Jade Buddha Temple** (p84) before a visit to **M50** (p86), where you can plug in to China's burgeoning modern-art scene. Still in a Buddhist frame of mind? Time for a meal at **Vegetarian Lifestyle** (p92).

☀ From **Jing'an Temple** (p92) it's only one stop on the metro to the French Concession West, where you can check out some of the area's more obscure sights, such as the **Propaganda Poster Art Centre** (p75) or the old villas along **Wukang Road** (p73). If Shanghai's consumerism beckons, be sure to check out local fashion boutiques such as **XinleLu.com** (p80).

☾ Time for dinner – **Yin** (p75) is good for a romantic night out, while Shanghainese classics **Jesse** (p77) and **Baoluo Jiulou** (p77) are sure to offer a more boisterous and lively atmosphere. You're in the right place to go out for a nightcap or hit the clubs; otherwise head back to Jing'an to spend an evening with the **acrobats** (p93).

Day Four

☀ Most of the city's main sights have been checked off the list by now, so today offers the opportunity to visit some lesser-known areas. Begin the day strolling through the busy streets of **Hongkou** (p44), which is also home to the **Ohel Moishe Synagogue** (p115) – now the Shanghai Jewish Refugees Museum.

☀ If you need a break from the city, hop on the metro for a trip out to **Qibao** (p102), an erstwhile canal town and popular destination for domestic tourists. Qibao has several low-key sights, but the main activity here is wandering among the old-style buildings – don't miss the old teahouse with its traditional (albeit incomprehensible) storytelling performance. For an entirely different experience, head to the **AP Xinyang Fashion and Gifts Market** (p119) to fish for fresh- and saltwater pearls or pick up bargain T-shirts and shoes.

☾ Time for one last blowout meal. For classy, old-fashioned ambience head to **Ye Shanghai** (p67) or **Fu 1039** (p76); alternatively, turn on the heat Sichuan-style with an evening at **Pinchuan** (p76) or **Yuxin Chuancai** (p38).

Need to Know

For more information,
see Survival Guide (p131).

Currency
Yuan (¥)

Language
Mandarin and Shanghainese

Visas
Thirty-day single-entry visa standard
for most nationalities. Longer visas are
available, but can be a hassle to obtain.

Money
ATMs are widely available; always
carry cash. High-end hotels, shops and
restaurants generally accept credit cards.

Mobile Phones
Inexpensive pay-as-you-go SIM cards are
available for unlocked GSM phones. If your
phone is not compatible, buying or renting a
local phone is a reasonable option.

Time
Chinese Standard Time (GMT/UTC plus
eight hours)

Plugs & Adaptors
Three main pin styles: three-pronged angle
pins (Australia), two flat pins (US, without the
ground), and two round pins (Europe). Three-
pronged round pins (Hong Kong) also exist.
Voltage is 220.

Tipping
Not practised in China. High-end restaurants
and hotels include a 15% service charge in the
bill, though hotel porters may expect a tip.

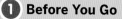

❶ Before You Go

Your Daily Budget

Budget less than ¥1400
► Dorm beds ¥55–¥65
► Double room at Chinese chain hotel
¥150–¥400
► Meal at mall food courts and tiny eateries ¥35

Midrange ¥1400–¥2000
► Double room ¥1000–¥1500
► Good local dinner ¥120
► Cocktail at local bar ¥70

Top End over ¥2000
► Luxury hotels ¥1500 and up
► Gastronomic dinner ¥300 and up

Useful Websites

Lonely Planet (www.lonelyplanet.com/
shanghai) Destination information, bookings,
traveller forum and more.

Smart Shanghai (www.smartshanghai.com)
Listings website.

Time Out (www.timeoutshanghai.com)
Listings website.

Explore Shanghai (www.exploreshanghai.com)
Phone-sized metro map.

Advance Planning

One month before Ensure visa and passport are in order. Check whether your trip
will coincide with festivals or holidays and
plan accordingly.

Two weeks before Consider possible itineraries and make restaurant reservations.

Two days before Learn how to count to 10
and say 'thank you' in Mandarin!

② Arriving in Shanghai

Shanghai has two main airports: Pudong International Airport and Hongqiao Airport. Unless you are flying in from elsewhere in China, you'll arrive at Pudong. The quickest and easiest transport options are listed below.

✈ From Pudong International Airport

Destination	Best Transport
Bund	Maglev, then taxi or metro line 2
People's Sq	Maglev, then taxi or metro line 2
Xintiandi (French Concession)	Maglev, then taxi
Jing'an Temple	Airport bus 2
Pudong (Lujiazui)	Maglev, then taxi or metro line 2

✈ From Hongqiao Airport

Destination	Best Transport
Bund	Metro lines 2 or 10
People's Sq	Metro line 2
Xintiandi (French Concession)	Metro line 10
Jing'an Temple	Metro line 2
Pudong (Lujiazui)	Metro line 2

🚕 Taxi

Taking a taxi from the Maglev terminus (Longyang Rd) is probably the fastest and easiest way into the city from Pudong International Airport. It should cost you ¥40 to ¥60 to downtown Shanghai.

③ Getting Around

Certain areas of Shanghai are more conducive to walking than others, but overall you should not expect enchanting European-style strolls here: walking through a Chinese city will wear you out faster than you expect. Although the metro is usually crowded, it's far and away the best way to get around.

Ⓜ Metro

Shanghai's continuously expanding metro system is indicated by a large red M. Lines 1, 2 and 10 are the most useful for travellers. Tickets cost between ¥3 and ¥10 depending on distance, and are sold from coin- and note-operated bilingual automated machines. Keep your ticket until you exit. One-/three-day metro passes are sold at the airports and from some information desks for ¥18/45. Most lines shut down by 10.30pm.

🚕 Taxi

Shanghai's taxis are reasonably cheap, hassle-free and easy to flag down outside rush hour, although finding a cab during rainstorms is impossible. Flag fall is ¥14 (for the first 3km) and ¥18 at night (11pm to 5am). To circumvent the language barrier, you *must* show the driver the Chinese address (included in this guide) of your destination.

Look for the meter when you get in the car; if the counter is hidden by a receipt, switch cabs or you will be heavily overcharged.

Shanghai Neighbourhoods

Worth a Trip
◉ **Top Sights**
Qibao

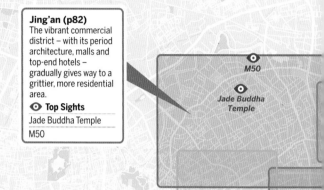

Jing'an (p82)

The vibrant commercial district – with its period architecture, malls and top-end hotels – gradually gives way to a grittier, more residential area.

◉ **Top Sights**

Jade Buddha Temple

M50

French Concession West (p70)

The western half of this area features some great dining and nightlife options along with low-key, leafy backstreets to explore.

The Bund & People's Square (p22)

Magnificent colonial-era buildings and a clutch of top-notch museums make downtown Shanghai the first stop on everybody's list.

⊙ Top Sights

The Bund

Shanghai Museum

Pudong (p96)

China's financial hub, Pudong is a dazzling panorama of high-altitude hotels, banks, Maglev trains and giant television screens.

The Bund ⊙

Shanghai Museum ⊙

⊙ *Yuyuan Gardens & Bazaar*

⊙ *Xintiandi*

Tianzifang ⊙

Old Town (p46)

The original city core and the only part to predate the 1850s, the Old Town is a glimpse of 'traditional' China.

⊙ Top Sights

Yuyuan Gardens & Bazaar

French Concession East (p56)

The most stylish part of town, the former French Concession is where the bulk of Shanghai's disposable income is spent.

⊙ Top Sights

Tianzifang

Xintiandi

Explore
Shanghai

Worth a Trip

Huxinting Teahouse, Yuyuan Gardens (p48)
PETER GRIDLEY/GETTY IMAGES ©

Explore

The Bund & People's Square

Shanghai's standout spectacle, the Bund has emerged in the past decade as a designer retail and dining zone, and the city's most exclusive boutiques, restaurants and hotels see the strip as the only place to be. Further west is People's Sq, the de facto city centre, home to a clutch of museums, entertainment venues, malls and leafy parks.

The Sights in a Day

☼ Rise with the sun for early-morning riverside views of the **Bund** (p24) as the city stirs from its slumber. Visit landmark buildings such as the Fairmont Peace Hotel and the HSBC building or follow the **walking tour** (p106) through the North Bund area. From here, explore **East Nanjing Road** (p32) like a local, stopping off for lunch at **South Memory** (p37), **Yuxin Chuancai** (p38) or one of the area's standout **dumpling options** (p38).

☼ E Nanjing Rd leads to People's Sq, known for its museums. The star attraction is the **Shanghai Museum** (p28) – you could easily spend the rest of the day here. Alternatively, the **Shanghai Urban Planning Exhibition Hall** (p36) makes for a fun browse.

☾ As evening falls, return to the Bund for dinner. Try **Lost Heaven** (p36) for Yunnanese, **el Willy** (p38) for Spanish or **Mr & Mrs Bund** (p38) for French bistro with a twist. Afterwards, head to any of the nearby bars for cocktails or take an evening river **cruise** (p113).

⊙ Top Sights

The Bund (p24)

Shanghai Museum (p28)

○ Local Life

East Nanjing Road (p32)

♥ Best of Shanghai

Eating

Lost Heaven (p36)

Yang's Fry Dumplings (p38)

Nanxiang Steamed Bun Restaurant (p38)

Yunnan Road Food Street (p37)

Mr & Mrs Bund (p38)

el Willy (p38)

Entertainment

Fairmont Peace Hotel Jazz Bar (p42)

Yifu Theatre (p42)

Shanghai Grand Theatre (p42)

Getting There

Ⓜ **Metro** The Bund is a 10-minute walk east from the E Nanjing Rd stop (lines 2 and 10). People's Sq station is served by lines 1, 2 and 8.

🚋 **Tourist Train** Runs the length of E Nanjing Rd's pedestrianised section (tickets ¥2) from Middle Henan Rd to the Shanghai No 1 Department Store.

Top Sights
The Bund

Symbolic of colonial Shanghai, the Bund (外滩) was the city's Wall St, a place of feverish trading and fortunes made and lost. Coming to Shanghai and missing the Bund is like visiting Beijing and bypassing the Forbidden City. Originally a towpath for dragging barges of rice, it's remained the first port of call for visitors since passengers began disembarking here over a century ago, although today it's the trendy restaurants and views of Pudong that beckon the crowds.

👁 Map p34, G2

E Zhongshan No 1 Rd; 中山东一路

Ⓜ E Nanjing Rd

The Bund

Don't Miss

The Promenade

The Bund offers a host of things to do, but most visitors head straight for the riverside promenade to pose for photos in front of Pudong's continually morphing skyline across the river. The 1km walkway can be accessed anywhere in between Huangpu Park (the northern end) and the Meteorological Signal Tower (the southern end).

Huangpu Park

China's first ever public park (1868) achieved lasting notoriety for its apocryphal 'No Dogs or Chinese Allowed' sign. The park today is blighted by the anachronistic Monument to the People's Heroes, which hides the entrance to the **Bund History Museum** (admission free; ☺9am-4pm Mon-Fri), where you'll find a small collection of old maps and photographs.

Jardine Matheson

Standing at No 27 is the former headquarters of early opium traders Jardine Matheson, which went on to become one of the most powerful trading houses in Hong Kong and Shanghai. Also known as EWO, it was the first foreign company to erect a building on the Bund in 1851. In 1941 the British Embassy occupied the top floor. Today it holds the House of Roosevelt, China's largest wine cellar and bar.

Bank of China

A glorious meld of Chinese and Western architectural styling, this 1940s building (No 23) is a neat collusion of art deco and Middle Kingdom motifs. Check out the funky modern-style Chinese lions out front. It was originally designed to be the tallest building in the city but wound up 1m shorter than its neighbour.

☑ **Top Tips**

▶ The promenade is open around the clock, but it's at its best in the early morning, when locals are out practising taichi, or in the early evening, when both sides of the river are lit up and the majesty of the waterfront is at its grandest.

▶ You can arrange an hour-long tour of the Bund's most famous monument, the Fairmont Peace Hotel, through the **Peace Gallery** (☎6321 6888, ext 6751; tours ¥100; ☺10am-7pm) in the lobby's mezzanine. Book a half-day in advance.

✖ **Take a Break**

There are plenty of fantastic drinking and dining options along the Bund, but if you're just looking for a low-key spot to get off your feet, try **Atanu** (1 E Zhongshan No 2 Rd; ☺10am-2am) in the Meteorological Signal Tower.

Fairmont Peace Hotel

Victor Sassoon built Shanghai's most treasured art deco monument in the late '20s, when it was known as the Cathay Hotel. It was frequented by well-heeled celebrities (from George Bernard Shaw to Charlie Chaplin) – the riff-raff slept elsewhere. You don't need to be a guest, though, to admire the wonderful art deco lobby and rotunda or listen to the old jazz band (p42).

Former Palace Hotel

The former Palace Hotel was China's largest hotel when completed (1909), and hosted Sun Yatsen's 1911 victory celebration following his election as the first president of the Republic of China. Now run by Swatch, it's home to an artist's residency program, with a gallery expected to open in the future.

Former Chartered Bank Building

Reopened in 2004 as the upscale entertainment complex Bund 18, the building boasts one of the Bund's premier late-night destinations: the top-floor Bar Rouge. The ground floor offers a sampler of the area's exclusive tastes, featuring luxury brands such as Cartier and Zegna.

North China Daily News Building

Known as the 'Old Lady of the Bund', the *News* ran from 1864 to 1951 as the main English-language newspaper in China. Look for the paper's motto above the central windows. The huge Atlas figures supporting the roof were designed in Italy and sculpted in Shanghai; each figure was carved from three blocks of granite.

Custom House

The Custom House (No 13), first established at this site in 1857 and rebuilt in 1927, has long been one of the most important buildings on the Bund. Capping the building is Big Ching, a bell modelled on London's Big Ben. During the Cultural Revolution, the bell was replaced with loudspeakers broadcasting revolutionary songs.

Hongkong & Shanghai Bank Building

Put a crick in your neck gawping at the ceiling mosaic portraying the 12 zodiac signs and the world's eight great banking centres. When it went up in 1923, the domed **HSBC building** (No 12; ⏱9am-4.30pm Mon-Fri) was the second-largest bank in the world and commonly known as 'the finest building east of Suez'.

Three on the Bund

With its opening in 2004, Three on the Bund became the strip's first lifestyle destination and the model that many other Bund edifices have since followed. Upscale restaurants and bars occupy the upper three floors, while the lower levels are anchored by Armani, the Evian Spa and the conceptually minded **Shanghai Gallery of Art** (⏱11am-9pm).

Meteorological Signal Tower

This **signal tower** (No 1; admission free; ⏱10am-5pm) was built in 1907 to replace the wooden original as well as to serve as a meteorological relay station for the tireless Shanghai Jesuits. The ground floor contains a small scattering of historical photographs, while the upper floors house the cafe Atanu.

Restaurants

There's no shortage of upscale Western restaurants here, many of which sport fabulous views. Top choices are Mr & Mrs Bund (p38) at Bund 18 and M on the Bund (p39). Lost Heaven (p36) has the finest Chinese cuisine in the area, though unfortunately no panoramas.

Nightlife

If cocktails are your thing, you're spoilt for choice: decadent watering holes include the Long Bar (p39), Glamour Bar (p39), New Heights (p39) and Bar Rouge (p41). The Fairmont Peace Hotel has its old-fashioned Jazz Bar (p42) and street-side cafe Victor's (p41). If pizza and beer is more your style, head to the Captain's Bar (p39) on Fuzhou Rd.

Top Sights
Shanghai Museum

An invigorating shot of adrenalin into the leaden legs of Chinese museum-goers, the Shanghai Museum (上海博物馆) houses a stupefying collection of the cream of the millennia, all under one roof. Exhibits cover the high watermarks of Chinese civilisation, from the meditative beauty of landscape paintings to the exquisite perfection of a celadon vase. Thorough English captions, a light-filled atrium and well-spaced exhibits are all arcs on an enticing learning curve.

◎ Map p34, C5

www.shanghaimuseum.net

201 Renmin Ave (entrance on E Yan'an Rd)

admission free

◷9am-5pm Mon-Fri (last entry 4pm)

Ⓜ People's Square

Shanghai Museum, designed by architect Xing Tonghe

Don't Miss

Ancient Chinese Bronzes Gallery

On the ground floor is the Shanghai Museum's star attraction, an unrivalled collection of ancient bronzes, some of which date as far back as the 21st century BC. The remarkable diversity of shapes is striking, revealing the significance of bronze in early society. Objects range from sacrificial vessels and wine jars to weapons and two-toned bells.

Ancient Chinese Sculpture Gallery

Also on the ground floor is this gallery, whose exhibits range from the funeral sculptures of the Qin and Han dynasties to the predominantly Buddhist sculptures of the following centuries, which were heavily influenced by the Indian and Central Asian styles that came to China via the Silk Road. A must for those interested in Buddhist artwork.

Ancient Chinese Ceramics Gallery

On the 2nd floor, this is one of the largest and most fascinating galleries in the museum. Don't worry if you don't know your 'ewer with overhead handles in *doucai*' from your 'brush-holder with *fencai* design'; it's all part of a magnificent introduction to this rich tradition. Highlights include the Tang tricolour pottery and Song-dynasty tableware.

Chinese Painting Gallery

This gallery leads visitors through various styles of traditional Chinese painting, from hanging and horizontal scrolls to album leaflets that depict nature in miniature. Look for works by masters such as Ni Zan (1301–74), Wang Meng (1308–85) and Qiu Ying (1494–1552), and compare the impressive array of brush techniques used over the centuries.

☑ **Top Tips**

▶ It's best to arrive in the morning, as only 8000 people are allowed in daily and the lines can quickly get long.

▶ Before you enter the museum, admire the exterior of the building. Designed to recall an ancient bronze *ding* (three-legged ritual vessel), the building also echoes the shape of a famous bronze mirror from the Han dynasty, exhibited within the museum.

▶ The audio guide is well worth the ¥40 fee (¥400 deposit, or your passport). It highlights particularly interesting items within an exhibit and offers good gallery overviews.

✗ **Take a Break**

There's a simple restaurant on the ground floor and a cafe on the 2nd floor if you need a break, but the best place for a real meal is outside the museum at the nearby Yunnan Road Food Street (p37).

Shanghai Museum

4th Floor

Minority Nationalities Art Gallery
Ancient Chinese Jade Gallery
Ming & Qing Furniture Gallery

3rd Floor

Chinese Painting Gallery
Chinese Calligraphy Gallery
Chinese Seal Gallery

2nd Floor

Ancient Chinese Ceramics Gallery
Café

Ground Floor

People's Square Exit
Ancient Chinese Bronzes Gallery
Ancient Chinese Sculpture Gallery
Audio Guides
Audio Guides
Gift Shop
Restaurant
Main Entrance

Chinese Calligraphy Gallery

Chinese characters, which express both meaning as a word and visual beauty as an image, are one of the language's most fascinating aspects. While the full scope of this gallery may be unfathomable for those who don't read Mandarin, anyone can enjoy the purely aesthetic balance of the brush artistry, much of which dates back hundreds of years.

Chinese Seal Gallery

Although obscure, this gallery provides a fascinating glimpse into the niche art form of miniature carving. Seals (chops) are notable both for the intricacy of their design and the special script used on the underside, which is known to only a handful of artisans and calligraphers. Look for the two orange soapstone seals that feature incredibly detailed landscapes in miniature.

Minority Nationalities Art Gallery

Save some energy for the Minority Nationalities Art Gallery, which introduces visitors to the diversity of China's non-Han ethnic groups, totalling (officially) some 40 million people. Displays focus mainly on dress, from the salmon fish-skin suit from Heilongjiang and the furs of the Siberian Oroqen, to the embroidery and batik of Guizhou's Miao and Dong.

Ming & Qing Furniture Gallery

This 4th-floor gallery features elegant rose- and sandalwood furniture from the Ming dynasty, and heavier, more baroque examples from the succeeding Qing dynasty. Several mock offices and reception rooms offer a glimpse of wealthy Chinese home life.

Ancient Chinese Jade Gallery

The most important precious stone in China, jade use dates back some 5000 years. This gallery introduces pieces such as early mystical totems and symbols (such as the *bi*, or 'jade discs', used to worship heaven), ritual weapons and jewellery. Bamboo drills, abrasive sand and garnets crushed in water were used to shape the pieces.

Local Life
East Nanjing Road

Running between the Bund and People's Sq is this shopping strip, which originally rose to prominence in the 1920s as the site of China's first department stores. A glowing forest of neon at night, it's no longer the cream of Shanghai shopping, but its pedestrian section is still one of the most famous and crowded streets in China.

❶ Noodles & Hotpot

Rising above the E Nanjing Rd metro station is the seven-storey **Hongyi Plaza** (宏伊国际广场; 299 E Nanjing Rd; 🕙10am-10pm), which anchors the eastern end of the pedestrian strip. While the shopping is nothing to crow about, there are some fabulous eating options here, which are always bustling at mealtimes. Head to the basement for snacks.

2 Yunhong Chopsticks Shop

One-stop chopstick shopping is sorted at this busy **store** (韵泓筷子店; 387 E Nanjing Rd; ⊙10am-10pm). Styles range from basic wooden models for so-so friends back home to solid silver sets (the precious metal dispels toxins) for your current crush.

3 China's Gap

Metersbonwe (美特斯邦威; 387 E Nanjing Rd; ⊙10am-10pm) has over 2000 retail outlets throughout the country. For those who want a peek at China's youth fashions – the brand is often compared to Gap and Zara – Shanghai's flagship store is the place to start.

4 Traditional Art

Duo Yun Xuan (朵云轩; 422 E Nanjing Rd; ⊙9.30am-9.30pm) is a traditional-looking building (look for the two enormous calligraphy brushes outside) with an excellent selection of art and calligraphy supplies. The 2nd floor is one of the best places for art books, while the 3rd floor houses antiques and some excellent calligraphy and brush-painting galleries.

5 Traditional Chinese Medicine

Opened in 1882, **Cai Tong De** (蔡同德; 450 E Nanjing Rd; ⊙9am-10pm) is one of the oldest and most famous traditional pharmacies in Shanghai. There's a clinic and herbal pharmacy on the top floor (no English), while the ground floor carries speciality items such as ginseng, caterpillar fungus and acupuncture supplies.

6 No 1 Food Store

This **store** (上海市第一食品商店; 720 E Nanjing Rd; ⊙10am-10pm) is bedlam, but this is how the Shanghainese shop and it's lots of fun. Trawl the ground floor for dried mushrooms, sea cucumbers, moon cakes and dried fruit. Built in 1926 and renovated in 2012, this used to be Sun Sun, one of Shanghai's big department stores.

7 Shanghai No 1 Department Store

Opened in 1936, this **department store** (上海市第一百货商店; 800 E Nanjing Rd; ⊙9.30am-10pm) was formerly known as the Sun Company and was one of E Nanjing Rd's big department stores (with Wing On, Sun Sun and Sincere) and the first equipped with an escalator. Today, it averages 150,000 shoppers a day.

8 Moore Memorial Church

This Methodist **church** (316 Middle Xizang Rd) was designed by legendary Shanghai architect Ladislaus Hudec in 1929. Hudec also designed the nearby **Park Hotel** (170 W Nanjing Rd), once Shanghai's tallest building.

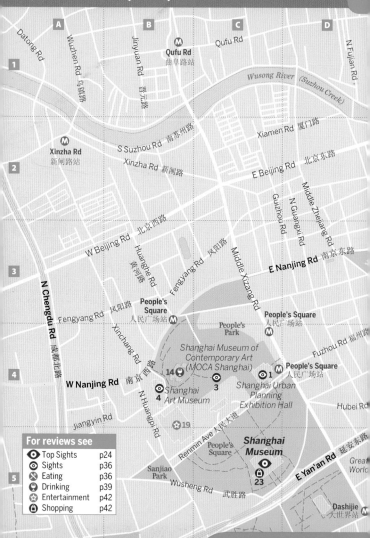

A B C D

Datong Rd

Wuzhen Rd 乌镇路

Jinyuan Rd 晋元路

Ⓜ Qufu Rd
曲阜路站

Qufu Rd

N Fujian Rd

1

Wusong River (Suzhou Creek)

Xiamen Rd 厦门路

Ⓜ Xinzha Rd
新闸路站

S Suzhou Rd 南苏州路

Xinzha Rd 新闸路

E Beijing Rd 北京东路

2

Guizhou Rd

N Guangxi Rd

Middle Zhejiang Rd

W Beijing Rd 北京西路

Huanghe Rd 黄河路

Fengyang Rd

Fengyang Rd 凤阳路

Middle Xizang Rd

E Nanjing Rd 南京东路

3

N Chengdu Rd 成都北路

Fengyang Rd

凤阳路

People's
Square
人民广场站 Ⓜ

People's Square
人民广场站 Ⓜ

Fuzhou Rd 福州路

People's
Square
人民广场 Ⓜ

People's
Park

W Nanjing Rd 南京西路

Xinchang Rd

N Huangpi Rd

Shanghai Museum of
Contemporary Art
(MOCA Shanghai)

People's Square
人民广场站 Ⓜ

4

◎ 14

◎ 3

◎ 1

Hubei Rd

◎ Shanghai
Art Museum

◎ 4

Shanghai Urban
Planning
Exhibition Hall

Jiangyin Rd

☆ 19

Renmin Ave 人民大道

Shanghai
Museum

E Yan'an Rd 延安东路

Great
World

Sanjiao
Park

People's
Square

Ⓛ 23

5

Wusheng Rd

武胜路

Dashijie
大世界站

Sights

Shanghai Urban Planning Exhibition Hall
MUSEUM

1 📍 Map p34, C?

...cities romanticise their past, ...promise good times in the ...t, but only in China are you ...d to visit places that haven't ...en built yet. The 3rd floor features Shanghai's idealised future, with an incredible model layout of the megalopolis-to-come plus a dizzying Virtual World 3-D wrap-around tour complete with celebratory fireworks. (上海城市规划展示馆; 100 Renmin Ave, entrance on Middle Xizang Rd; 人民大道100号; admission ¥30; ⏰9am-5pm Tue-Sun, last entry 4pm; Ⓜ People's Square)

Rockbund Art Museum
MUSEUM

2 📍 Map p34, G1

Housed in the former Royal Asiatic Society building (1933), this private museum behind the Bund focuses on contemporary Chinese art, with rotating exhibits year-round. Opened in 2010 to mark the opening of the Rockbund (North Bund) renovation project, the museum has since become one of the city's top modern-art venues. (上海外滩美术馆; www.rockbundartmuseum.org; 20 Huqiu Rd; 虎丘路20号; admission ¥15; ⏰10am-6pm Tue-Sun; Ⓜ E Nanjing Rd)

Shanghai Museum of Contemporary Art (MOCA Shanghai)
MUSEUM

3 📍 Map p34, C4

With its all-glass construction squeezing every last photon from Shanghai's murky sunlight, this independent museum is doing a cracking job of bringing contemporary international artwork to the city. (上海当代艺术馆; www.mocashanghai.org; People's Park; 人民公园; admission ¥30; ⏰10am-9.30pm; Ⓜ People's Square)

Shanghai Art Museum
MUSEUM

4 📍 Map p34, B4

The modern Chinese art exhibits are hit and miss, but the building (the former Shanghai Racecourse Club) and its period details are simply gorgeous. (上海美术馆; www.sh-artmuseum.org.cn; 325 W Nanjing Rd; 南京西路325号; admission free; ⏰9am-5pm, last entry 4pm; Ⓜ People's Square)

Eating

Lost Heaven
YUNNANESE $$$

5 🍴 Map p34, H4

Lost Heaven might not have the views that keep its rivals in business, but why go to the same old Western restaurants when you can get sophisticated Bai, Dai and Miao folk cuisine from China's mighty southwest? Specialities are flowers (banana and pomegranate), wild mushrooms, chillies, Burmese

Zhang Huan's *Q Confucius No.2* (2011) at Rockbund Art Museum

curries, Bai chicken and superb *pu'erh* (aged fermented tea from Yunnan), all served up in gorgeous Yunnan-meets-Shanghai surrounds. Reserve. (花马天堂; ☑ 6330 0967; www.lostheaven.com.cn; 17 E Yan'an Rd; 延安东路17号; dishes ¥38-180; Ⓜ E Nanjing Rd)

Yunnan Road Food Street
CHINESE $

6 🍴 Map p34, E5

This is just the spot for an authentic meal after museum-hopping at People's Sq. Look out for Shaanxi dumplings at No 15, salted duck (盐水鸭) at No 55, five-fragrance dim sum at No 28 and Mongolian hotpot. (云南南路美食街; S Yunnan Rd; 云南南路; Ⓜ People's Square)

South Memory
HUNANESE $$

7 🍴 Map p34, F2

One of the standout choices in the popular Hongyi Plaza, this Hunanese restaurant features tantalising spicy dry pots (served in a personal mini wok), such as bamboo shoots and smoked pork or chicken and chestnuts. Arrive early for a window seat; alternatively, try Hong Kong–style **Charme** on the 3rd floor or Japanese noodle fave **Ajisen** in the basement. (望湘园; 6th fl, Hongyi Plaza, 299 E Nanjing Rd; 南京东路299号宏伊国际广场6楼; Ⓜ E Nanjing Rd)

Yuxin Chuancai

SICHUANESE $$

8 🍴 Map p34, E3

A regular contender for one of Shanghai's best Sichuanese restaurants, Yuxin pulls no punches when it comes to the blistering chillies and numbing peppercorns. Menu all-stars include the 'mouthwatering chicken' starter (口水鸡), spicy frog legs, tea-smoked duck, hot-stone beef and catfish in chilli oil. (渝信川菜; 5th fl, Huasheng Tower, 399 Jiujiang Rd; 九江路399号华盛大厦5楼; dishes ¥18-98; M E Nanjing Rd)

Shanghai Grandmother

CHINESE $

9 🍴 Map p34, G3

This packed home-style eatery is within easy striking distance of the

Local Life
Best Dumplings

There's no better-tasting introduction to Shanghainese cuisine.

Yang's Fry Dumplings (Map p34, B3; 小杨生煎馆; 101 Huanghe Rd; 黄河路101号; per 4 dumplings ¥6; M People's Square) The city's most popular fried dumplings (生煎; *shengjian*), coated with scallions and sesame seeds.

Nanxiang Steamed Bun Restaurant (Map p34, D4; 南翔馒头店; 2nd fl, 666 Fuzhou Rd; 福州路666号2楼; steamer 8 dumplings ¥25-50; M People's Square) Modern branch of Shanghai's most famous steamed-dumpling restaurant.

Bund and perfect for a casual lunch or dinner. You can't go wrong with the classics here: the fried tomato and egg, Grandmother's braised pork and three-cup chicken will ease you into Shanghai dining. (上海姥姥; ☎6321 6613; 70 Fuzhou Rd; 福州路70号; dishes ¥20-52; M E Nanjing Rd)

Mr & Mrs Bund

FRENCH $$$

10 🍴 Map p34, G2

Paul Pairet opened this casual eatery in 2008, aiming for a space that's considerably more playful than your average fine-dining restaurant. The mix-and-match menu has a heavy French bistro slant, but re-imagined and served up with Pairet's ingenious presentation. Reserve. (☎6323 9898; www.mmbund.com; 6th fl, Bund 18, 18 E Zhongshan No 1 Rd; 中山东一路18号6楼; mains ¥150-600; ⊙lunch & dinner, to 4am Tue-Sat; M E Nanjing Rd)

el Willy

SPANISH $$$

11 🍴 Map p34, H4

The unstoppable energy of colourful-sock-wearing Barcelona chef Willy fuels this new South Bund space, which ups its charms with a bold selection of creative tapas and cool river views through the 5th-floor arched windows. Reserve. (☎5404 5757; www.el-willy.com; 5th fl, 22 E Zhongshan No 2 Rd; 中山东二路22号5楼; tapas ¥45-165, rice for 2 ¥195-265; ⊙Mon-Sat; taxi)

M on the Bund

CONTINENTAL $$$

12 Map p34, H3

The first to pitch up on the waterfront in the closing years of the last millennium, Michelle Garnaut's winning M on the Bund restaurant remains as crisp as its white linen. The food is Continental (crispy suckling pig, *magret de canard*), complemented by a gorgeous art deco interior and 7th-floor terrace. Reserve. (6350 9988; www.m-onthebund.com; 7th fl, 20 Guangdong Rd; 广东路20号7楼; mains ¥188-288; ME Nanjing Rd)

Drinking

Glamour Bar

BAR

Comfortably gorgeous, Michelle Garnaut's bar moved down a floor from M on the Bund (see **12** Map p34, H3), and up the wish list of Shanghai socialites. A steady flow of elegant people enjoy tantalising martinis at the window seats midweek, avoiding the weekend crush. Great events line-up. (魅力酒吧; 6th fl, 20 Guangdong Rd; 广东路20号6楼; 5pm-late; ME Nanjing Rd)

Long Bar

BAR

13 Map p34, H3

For a taste of colonial-era Shanghai's elitist trappings, you'll do no better than the gorgeous Long Bar inside the Waldorf Astoria. This was once the members-only Shanghai Club, whose most spectacular accoutrement was a 34m-long wooden bar, said to be the longest in Asia. (廊吧; 2 E Zhongshan No 1 Rd; 中山东一路2号; 4pm-1am; ME Nanjing Rd)

Barbarossa

BAR

14 Map p34, B4

The implausible Moroccan vibe of this secluded bar eagerly taps into Shanghai's eclectic desires. Its inviting ground-floor dining area gives way to an oasis of scattered cushions, hookah pipes and a terrace bar upstairs, and the music is set to chill. Target happy hour (5pm to 8pm) to elude staggering prices. (芭芭露莎会所餐厅; People's Park, 231 W Nanjing Rd; 南京西路231号, 人民公园内; 11am-2am; MPeople's Square)

New Heights

BAR

15 Map p34, H3

The most amenable of the big Bund bars, this splendid terrace has the choicest angle on Pudong's hypnotising neon performance. (新视角; 7th fl, Three on the Bund, 3 E Zhongshan No 1 Rd; 中山东一路3号外滩3号7楼; 11am-1.30am; ME Nanjing Rd)

Captain's Bar

BAR

16 Map p34, G3

There's the odd drunken sailor, and the crummy lift needs updating here at the Captain's Bar. But it is a fine Bund-side terrace-equipped bar for phosphorescent Pudong views – as long as rubbing shoulders with the preening glitterati and the desperate-to-impress isn't a must. (船长青年酒吧;

Understand

Opium Trade & the Foreign Concessions

Although Shanghai had served as a port city since the 14th century, the seeds of its future as an international trading hub were not sown until the late 18th century, when British traders based in Canton (Guangzhou) began importing opium to trade for silver, thus correcting a marked trade imbalance. The highly addictive drug rapidly permeated all levels of Chinese society, with *hongs* (trading houses) such as Jardine Matheson built upon its trade.

Smouldering friction between Great Britain and China over the drug finally erupted in the conflict fought in its name: the First Opium War. The Treaty of Nanking (1842) that concluded the hostilities opened five ports, including Shanghai and Canton, to the West.

The Concessions

Of the five ports, Shanghai was the most prosperous due to its superb geographical location, capital edge and marginal interference from the Chinese government. Great Britain's arrival in Shanghai, dating from 1843, was soon followed by that of other nations. Trade quickly flourished as the area outside the Old Town was divided into British, French and American Concessions. The original British Concession included the Bund and the area extending due west to today's People's Sq; the American Concession was established shortly thereafter to the north in Hongkou. These two concessions later joined to form one large area known as the International Settlement. The French settlement began to the south with a small sliver of land wedged between the British Concession and the Chinese town (now the Old Town) but later developed inland, eventually giving rise to the area still known by foreigners as the French Concession.

Growth

Trade of silk, tea, textiles, porcelain and opium was matched by rapidly developing banking, insurance and real-estate sectors. China and the West traded with each other via Chinese middlemen called compradors (from the Portuguese). Lured by the sense of opportunity, a growing swell of immigrants from other parts of China began to arrive. The city found itself propelled into a new era of gaslight, electricity and cars, and became the foremost agent of modernisation and change in post-imperial China.

6th fl, 37 Fuzhou Rd; 福州路37号6楼; ⏰11am-2am; 🔊; Ⓜ E Nanjing Rd)

Bar Rouge

BAR

Bathed in ruby-red light and subdued by chill-out music and dazzling Pudong terrace views, high-profile Bar Rouge, above Mr & Mrs Bund (see 10 ✖ Map p34, G2), aims its seductive formula and superb cocktails at the moneyed crowd and 20-something fashionistas. (7th fl, Bund 18, 18 E Zhongshan No 1 Rd; 外滩18号7楼; ⏰6pm-2am Sun-Thu, to 4.30am Fri & Sat; Ⓜ E Nanjing Rd)

Victor's

CAFE

17 🚇 Map p34, G2

When you need a break from the push and pull of the Bund, refuel at this exceedingly *réposant* French cafe, whose large windows overlook E Nanjing Rd. It's pricey, but there's no faulting the location in the lobby of the Fairmont Peace Hotel, or the menu of quiches, salads, freshly baked pastries and coffee. (西饼屋; Fairmont Peace Hotel, 20 E Nanjing Rd; 南京东路20号; ⏰7am-10pm; Ⓜ E Nanjing Rd)

LONELY PLANET/GETTY IMAGES ©

Bar Rouge

M1nt

CLUB

18 ⬛ Map p34, F3

Exclusive penthouse-style club with knockout views, snazzy food and not a lot of dance space. Dress to impress or you'll get thrown into the shark tank. (24th fl, 318 Fuzhou Rd; 福州路318号24楼; ⊘lounge 6pm-late daily, club 9pm-late Wed-Sat; Ⓜ E Nanjing Rd)

Entertainment

Fairmont Peace Hotel Jazz Bar

JAZZ

Shanghai's most famous hotel features Shanghai's most famous jazz band, a septuagenarian sextet that's been churning out nostalgic covers such as 'Summertime' since time immemorial. The original band takes the stage from 7pm to 9.45pm; afterwards it's Theo Croker's smokin' **contemporary group** (⊘10pm-1am Tue-Sat). Entrance is ¥100; reserve on weekends. You'll pass Victor's (see **17** Map p34, G2) on the way in. (费尔蒙和平饭店爵士吧; ☑6138 6883; 20 E Nanjing Rd; 南京东路20号; ⊘5.30pm-1am; Ⓜ E Nanjing Rd)

Shanghai Grand Theatre

CLASSICAL MUSIC

19 ⭐ Map p34, B4

Shanghai's state-of-the-art concert venue hosts everything from Broadway musicals to symphonies, ballets, operas and performances by internationally acclaimed classical soloists.

Local Life
Chinese Opera

Just east of People's Sq, the **Yifu Theatre** (Map p34, D4; 逸夫舞台; ☑6322 5294; www.tianchan.com; 701 Fuzhou Rd; 福州路701号; Ⓜ People's Square) has Kunqu and Yue (Shaoxing) opera on the program, with a Beijing opera highlights show performed several times a week at 1.30pm and 7.15pm. Pick up a brochure at the ticket office.

Pick up a schedule at the ticket office. (上海大剧院; ☑6386 8686; www.shgtheatre.com; 300 Renmin Ave; 人民大道300号; Ⓜ People's Square)

Muse

CLUB

20 ⭐ Map p34, G1

One of the hottest clubs in the city for over six years now – and that's no small feat – Muse has moved downtown to this swanky Bund-side location. Don't go looking for a lot of dance space; just squeeze into the crowd or jump up on a private table (minimum ¥4000 per night). (5th fl, Yi Feng Galleria, 99 E Beijing Rd; 北京东路99号5楼; Ⓜ E Nanjing Rd)

Shopping

Annabel Lee

FASHION

21 🔒 Map p34, G3

An elegant shop with a gorgeous range of soft-coloured and playfully designed accessories in silk, linen and cashmere, many of which feature delicate and stylish embroidery. (安梨; No 1, Lane 8, E Zhongshan No 1 Rd; 中山东一路8弄1号; ⏱10am-10pm; Ⓜ E Nanjing Rd)

Suzhou Cobblers
SHOES

22 🔒 Map p34, G3

This micro outlet plies dainty, hand-embroidered silk slippers and shoes and also has a range of colourful bags, hats and lanterns. (上海起想艺术品; Unit 101, 17 Fuzhou Rd; 福州路17号101室; ⏱10am-6.30pm; Ⓜ E Nanjing Rd)

Shanghai Museum Art Store
SOUVENIRS, ARTS & CRAFTS

23 🔒 Map p34, C5

Save energy after seeing the Shanghai Museum for this emporium. Items include facsimiles of the museum's porcelain collection, reasonably priced prints, and postcards and books on Chinese art, architecture, travel and language. (上海博物馆艺术品商店; 201 Renmin Ave, entrance on E Yan'an Rd; 人民大道201号; ⏱9.30am-5pm; Ⓜ People's Square)

Shiatzy Chen
FASHION

One of the top names in Asian haute couture, Taiwanese designer Shiatzy Chen finds her inspiration in traditional Chinese aesthetics. The exclusive collections at her Bund 9 flagship store display a painstaking attention to detail and cross cultural boundaries with grace. It's around the corner from Suzhou Cobblers (see **22** 🔒 Map p34, G3). (夏姿; 9 E Zhongshan No 1 Rd; 中山东一路9号; Ⓜ E Nanjing Rd)

Blue Shanghai White
CERAMICS

This petite shop next to Suzhou Cobblers (see **22** 🔒 Map p34, G3) has a delightful collection of exquisite hand-painted ceramics, including porcelain teacups, teapots and vases. (海晨; Unit 103, 17 Fuzhou Rd; 福州路17号103房; ⏱10.30am-6.30pm; Ⓜ E Nanjing Rd)

Local Life
Hongkou

Getting There

Hongkou is located north of the Bund.

Ⓜ Metro North Sichuan Rd (line 10) is the closest station.

Originally the American Settlement and later the Japanese district, Hongkou is decidedly working class today, with many residents originating from nearby provinces such as Anhui and Jiangsu. It's somewhat rundown and grittier than other areas of Shanghai, but the lack of polish means there's plenty of interesting street life and older buildings waiting for discovery.

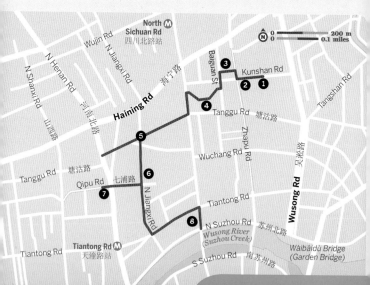

❶ Hongkew Methodist Church

This 1923 **church** (景灵堂; 135 Kunshan Rd; 昆山路135号) is where General Chiang Kaishek married Song Meiling (May-ling) in 1927. Meiling's father, Charlie, preached here briefly before he went into business as a printer. It's closed to the public, but the caretaker is quite friendly and will probably let you in.

❷ Young Allen Court

West along Kunshan Rd on the corner with Zhapu Rd stands this distinctive brick **building** (260 Zhapu Rd), constructed in 1923. Walk down the side of the alley for views of its three-storey architecture and the rear of the adjacent church towards the end.

❸ Shikumen Houses

This *lilong* (alley; No 13, the first on your left) doesn't look like anything special from the outside, but a wander down will reveal a row of eight decorative lintels, some of which are still fronted by the traditional black wooden doors of *shikumen* (stone-gate) homes.

❹ Art Deco Apartment Block

Near the intersection of Kunshan Rd and Baiguan St is a 1932 art deco apartment block. It stands adjacent to a line of grey-and-red-brick row houses, notable for their arched windows.

❺ Tanggu Road Food Market

Chinese markets always make for a fascinating stroll, though in Shanghai they can be hard to find unless you know where to look. This reliable spot is open throughout the day; you'll find all manner of things for sale, including thousand-year-old eggs, pickled vegetables, cured bacon, and live crabs and turtles.

❻ North Jiangxi Road

This is another fun strip, always alive with action. Scooters push through the crowds of pedestrians, while the street sides are lined with vendors selling fresh sugar-cane juice, stinky tofu and other snacks. Note the distinctive old house at No 174, allegedly the residence of Lotus, a gangster-police inspector's concubine, with the traditional characters 爱莲坊 (Love Lotus Residence) above the door.

❼ Clothing Market

Qipu Market (七浦服装市场; 168 & 183 Qipu Rd; 七浦路168 & 183号; ⏱7am-5pm) is where the masses come shopping for clothes and shoes. Consisting of two rabbit warren–like department stores surrounding the N Henan Rd intersection, it's one big 'everything must go now' sale. Haggle hard.

❽ Post Museum

It may sound like a yawner, but this is actually a pretty good **museum** (上海邮政博物馆; 250 N Suzhou Rd; ⏱9am-5pm Wed, Thu, Sat & Sun), where you can learn about postal history in imperial China and view rare stamps (1888–1978). It's located in a magnificent 1924 post office, with views from the rooftop garden (closed at time of writing).

Explore

Old Town

Shanghai's Old Town, known to locals as Nan Shi (Southern City), is an intriguing area of old-fashioned textures, tatty charm and musty temples, and is a favourite stop for visitors. The circular layout still reflects the footprint of the former city walls, flung up in the 16th century to defend against marauding Japanese pirates.

The Sights in a Day

Pre-empt the crowds by arriving at **Yuyuan Gardens** (p48) as it opens at 8.30am. After visiting the gardens, exit into Yuyuan Bazaar and consider a cup of tea at the Huxinting Teahouse or a short wander amid the souvenir shops and endless bustle of the market area. From here, find Chenxiangge Nunnery and take a **walking tour** (p50) of the nearby temples, alleyways and antique markets – don't forget to break for lunch at **Din Tai Fung** (p53) or **Songyuelou** (p55).

Finish the tour with a browse through the **Shiliupu Fabric Market** (p51), which specialises in tailor-made clothing. From here, you can catch a taxi over to the **Confucius Temple** (p53) and explore its surrounding alleyways, which are much less touristy than the area around the Yuyuan Bazaar. Continue on to the **Flower, Bird, Fish & Insect Market** (p53) and then the **Dongtai Road Antique Market** (p55) for a final round of souvenir shopping.

The outdoor terrace at **Fat Olive** (p55) is a good pick for pre- or post-dinner drinks.

👁 Top Sights

Yuyuan Gardens & Bazaar (p48)

🔍 Local Life

Backstreets & Alleyways (p50)

💜 Best of Shanghai

Temples & Churches
Chenxiangge Nunnery (p50)

Confucius Temple (p53)

Temple of the Town God (p49)

Markets & Antiques
Old Street (p51)

Shiliupu Fabric Market (p51)

Dongtai Road Antique Market (p55)

Fuyou Antique Market (p51)

Eating
Din Tai Fung (p53)

Songyuelou (p55)

Getting There

Ⓜ Metro Line 10 runs through the Old Town. Yuyuan Garden station is close to most sights.

🚲 Pedicabs Unofficial pedicabs sometimes hang out in the streets leading off the Bund; they'll take you directly to Yuyuan Gardens for ¥10 (total, not per person).

Top Sights
Yuyuan Gardens & Bazaar

With their shaded alcoves, pavilions, glittering pools churning with carp, and pines sprouting wistfully from rockeries, the Yuyuan Gardens (豫园) are one of Shanghai's premier sights – but they can be overpoweringly crowded at weekends. The surrounding streets and Buddhist and Taoist temples are among the few places in the city that retain a flavour of yesteryear, so if you're in need of an antidote to Shanghai's continuous quest for modernity, this is the place to come.

👁 Map p52, C2

Yuyuan Bazaar; 豫园商城

admission ¥40

🕗 8.30am-5.30pm, last entry 5pm

Ⓜ Yuyuan Garden

Pavilion in Yuyuan Gardens

Don't Miss

Origins

Founded between 1559 and 1577 by the well-to-do Pan family, these classical Chinese gardens are a fine example of Ming-dynasty design, although they were ransacked during both the Opium War and the Taiping Rebellion. Note the ingenious use of alcoves, windows and doorways, which lends an impression of size to a relatively small area.

Garden Highlights

Keep an eye out for the Great Rockery and Sansui Hall, two of the first sights you will encounter upon entering the garden. Another curiosity is the Exquisite Jade Rock, which was bound for the imperial court in Beijing until the boat sank off Shanghai. Also look for the Hall of Heralding Spring, which in 1853 was the headquarters for the Small Swords Society, and the beautiful stage (1888), with its gilded carved ceiling.

Yuyuan Bazaar

Surrounding the gardens is the **Yuyuan Bazaar** (豫园商城; Fuyou Rd), a bustling maze of souvenir stalls and famous snack shops. You won't be able to escape the fake Rolex vendors, but shopping here is nevertheless entertaining. Join the crowds surrounding the *layangpian* (拉洋片; peephole theatre) performer and don't forget to haggle.

Temple of the Town God

Chinese towns traditionally had a community of Taoist gods (often presided over by a main town god), who kept the populace from harm. This **temple** (城隍庙; Middle Fangbang Rd; admission ¥10; ⊙8.30am-4.30pm), accessed from Middle Fangbang Rd, originally dated to the early 15th century before being badly damaged during the Cultural Revolution.

☑ Top Tips

▶ Classical Chinese gardens were not designed to accommodate over a thousand visitors a day. For the best experience, make sure you get here at opening time, before the tour buses arrive.

▶ Pick up a map of the surrounding Yuyuan Bazaar at the **Tourist Information and Service Centre** (旅游咨询服务中心; 149 Jiujiaochang Rd; ⊙9am-7pm), near the intersection with Old St.

✕ Take a Break

Next to the garden entrance is the **Huxinting Teahouse** (湖心亭; ⊙8.30am-9.30pm), once part of the gardens and now one of the most famous teahouses in China. Its zigzag causeway, which can confuse visitors, is designed to thwart evil spirits, who can only travel in straight lines.

Local Life
Backstreets & Alleyways

The Old Town is a fascinating place to wander, particularly because it is one of the last bastions of traditional life in Shanghai. Real-estate development encroaches on what remains of the neighbourhood, but sneak into a back alley and you can still get a glimpse of life as it was 60 years ago.

❶ Chenxiangge Nunnery

Seek out the tidy floral courtyard at the rear of this delightful **retreat** (沉香阁; 29 Chenxiangge Rd; admission ¥10; ⏰7am-4pm; **M**Yuyuan Garden), with its muttered prayers and brown-clothed Buddhist nuns, to climb the **Guanyin Tower** (admission ¥2; ⏰7am-3pm), housing a compassionate effigy of the goddess of mercy, carved from *chenxiang* wood and seated in *lalitasana* (seated half-lotus) posture.

2 Wangyima Alley

Bypass the lion's share of the souvenir free-for-all outside the temple by following this twisting alleyway. You'll still find carved gourds and pseudo antiques alongside the sizzle of woks and makeshift noodle stands, but the shops soon give way to doting grandparents and banners of drying laundry. It's a veritable maze; look out for Zhongwang Yima Alley (中王医马弄) and turn right.

3 Old Street

The morass of Mao-era keepsakes brings no surprises, but the ye olde China streetscape of **Old Street** (老街; Middle Fangbang Rd) – once a canal – is entertaining. Vendors are tamer than at Yuyuan Bazaar, and there's a glut of souvenirs: shadow puppets, calendar posters, Yixing teapots, Tibetan jewellery, calligraphy scrolls and kites.

4 Antique Hunting

There's a permanent antique market here on the 1st and 2nd floors, but the **Fuyou Antique Market** (福佑工艺品市场; 459 Middle Fangbang Rd; M Yuyan Garden) really gets humming for the 'ghost market' on weekends, when sellers from the countryside fill up all four floors and then some. Mornings are best.

5 Tea Time

Dropping in at the **Old Shanghai Teahouse** (老上海茶馆; 385 Middle Fangbang Rd; ⏱9am-9pm; M Yuyuan Garden) is much

like barging into someone's attic, where ancient gramophones, records, typewriters and other period clutter share space with the aroma of Chinese tea and tempting snacks.

6 Return to the Alleyways

Pass the Temple of the Town God (p49) and then turn left to return to the Old Town's quiet alleyways, with their hanging laundry, bicycle bells and outdoor Chinese chess and mah jong games. Note the lovely old doorways on Danfeng Rd, such as the carved red-brick gateway at No 193.

7 Middle Fangbang Road

Note the old stone archway when you turn back onto Middle Fangbang Rd. These archways, known as *pailou* or *paifang*, originally marked the entrance to local communities within a larger neighbourhood. Middle Fangbang Rd remains a boisterous shopping street, filled with snack stands, clothing stores and booming stereo systems.

8 Tailored Clothing

Head to the **Shiliupu Fabric Market** (十六铺面料城; 2 Zhonghua Rd; ⏱8.30am-6.30pm; M Xiaonanmen) to browse for inexpensive silk, cashmere, wool, linen and cotton, but watch you don't wind up with a synthetic. Tailored clothing is a steal if you've got a silk shirt or traditional Chinese jacket on your shopping list – count on one to three days' turnaround.

A **B** **C** **D**

E Yan'an Rd 延安东路

S Yunnan Rd 云南南路

Yongshou Rd 永寿路

E Ninghai Rd 宁海东路

S Fujian Rd 宁海东路

E Jinling Rd 金陵东路

Middle Henan Rd 河南中路

Renmin Rd 人民路

Huángpǔ River

E Zhongshan No 2 Rd 中山东二路

Zhonghua Rd 中华路

1

M Dashijie 大世界站

Yuyuan Garden 豫园站 M

Fuyou Rd

Yuyuan Gardens & Bazaar

E Huaihai Rd 淮海东路

Chenxiangge Rd

Jiujiaochang Rd 旧校场路

福佑路

5 ⊗
⊗**6**

Anren St 安仁街

Wutong Rd 梧桐路

Danfeng Rd

Zhonghua Rd 中华路

2

Dajing Pavilion
3 ◎

Dajing Rd 大境路

Qingliang St

S Henan Rd 河南南路

Old St 老街

Zihua Rd

Middle Fangbang Rd 方浜中路

4 ⊗

7 ⓐ

Shouning Rd

Renmin Rd 人民路

OLD TOWN (NÁNSHÌ)

W Fangbang Rd

Zhoujin Rd

Xueyuan Rd 学院路

Huiji Rd

8 ⓐ

Dongtai Rd 东台路

Liuhekou Rd

ⓐ**2**

Flower, Bird, Fish & Insect Market

Jinjia Fang 金家坊

E Fuxing Rd 复兴东路

复兴东路

S Henan Rd 河南南路

Wangyun Rd 望云路

S Guangqi Rd

Xundao St 巡道街

Zizhong Rd

Laoximen 老西门站 M

Jingxiu Rd

Zhuangjia St

3

E Fuxing Rd 复兴东路

S Xizang Rd 西藏南路

Menghua St

Confucius Temple **1** ◎

Wenmiao Rd 文庙路

Pengjia Rd 蓬莱路

Zhonghua Rd 中华路

Shangwen Rd 尚文路

4

Zhizaoju Rd 制造局路

E Jianguo Rd

Daji Rd

Daxing St 大兴街

For reviews see

◎ Top Sights p48
◎ Sights p53
⊗ Eating p53
ⓐ Drinking p55
ⓐ Shopping p55

Dalin Rd

5

Lujiabang Rd 陆家浜路

M **Lujiabang Rd** 陆家浜路站

Nanchezhan Rd

W Puyu Rd

Puyu Donglu

Sights

Confucius Temple
TEMPLE

1  Map p52, B4

This well-tended shrine to Kongfuzi (Confucius) is pleasantly cultivated with hectares of pines and magnolias, amid birdsong. The temple is typically Confucian (introspective, retiring, quiet), but a busy second-hand book market of (largely Chinese-language) books gets going every Sunday morning. (文庙; 215 Wenmiao Rd; 文庙路215号; admission ¥10; ⏰9am-5pm; ⓂLaoximen)

Flower, Bird, Fish & Insect Market
MARKET

2 Map p52, A3

One of the few remaining traditional markets in town, this is the spot to go shopping for city-sized pets. There are all sorts of critters for sale, but it's the crickets and their bamboo cages that are the most remarkable. (万商花鸟鱼虫市场; S Xizang Rd; 西藏南路; ⏰9am-4pm; ⓂLaoximen)

Dajing Pavilion
PAVILION

3 Map p52, A2

Dating from 1815, this pavilion is attached to the sole preserved (and restored) section of the Old Town wall, which was toppled in 1912. On the ground floor is a Chinese-language exhibition of the Old Town, and you can climb the battlements. (大境阁; Dajing Rd; 大境路; admission ¥5; ⏰9am-4pm; ⓂDashijie)

Eating

Din Tai Fung
DUMPLINGS $$

4 Map p52, C2

If you love dumplings but aren't confident about eating street food, DTF is your spot. Styles run from crinkled *shaomai* to Shanghai's *xiaolongbao* (steamed dumplings), as well as vegetarian and other options. (鼎泰丰; www.dintaifungsh.com.cn; 2nd fl, Yu Fashion Garden, 168 Middle Fangbang Rd; 方浜中路168号豫龙坊2楼; dumplings ¥58-88; ⏰10.30am-10pm; ✏; ⓂYuyuan Garden)

BRADLEY MAYHEW/GETTY IMAGES ©

Statue at Confucius Temple

Understand

Life as a Shanghai Resident

Shanghai has a strong regional identity, forged from its unique history, dialect and geographic location. In many respects, however, the Shanghainese are similar to the Hong Kong Chinese: both are southern Chinese from flourishing coastal towns that historically served as havens for refugees and embraced Western customs and beliefs. Like the Hong Kong Chinese, the Shanghainese typically are physically shorter and thinner than their taller and stockier northern brethren.

The Shanghainese are admired by other Chinese for their competence and envied for their material successes. On the downside, they are also sometimes seen by their compatriots as being stingy, petty, calculating, unfriendly and demanding.

Shanghai has long flirted with the Western perspective, but the city remains staunchly Chinese in its traditions and customs. Like all Chinese, the Shanghainese are proud of their ancestry; concessions to Western taste are often no more than a theatrical device. The average Shanghai resident actually has little exposure to the West beyond the TV set, and speaks no English. It's easy to overlook, but virtually no tourists left China prior to 1979 and only in very recent years have visitor numbers to foreign destinations slowly grown. China – including Shanghai – remains comparably sheltered from the outside world.

Employment, health care, education and property prices are major concerns for both young families and retired workers. House prices have rocketed since the 1990s and although property prices on average are not as high as those in Europe or the US, the average salaries in Shanghai are far, far lower. With vast salary disparities and no ways to effect political change, the Shanghainese can do little but harness their ambitions. According to a local headhunter, well-paid white-collar employees can make anywhere from ¥50,000 to ¥90,000 (around US$7900 to US$14,300) a month, compared with a cashier, who might make ¥2500 (US$400), or someone earning minimum wage, who only makes ¥1450 (US$230) a month.

Nanxiang Steamed Bun Restaurant
DUMPLINGS $$

5 🍴 Map p52, C2

Shanghai's most celebrated pork and crabmeat *xiaolongbao* eatery is alas hugely popular – the takeaway queue emerging from the door says it all. There's a minimum per-person eat-in charge. (南翔馒头店; 85 Old Yuyuan Rd, Yuyuan Bazaar; 豫园商城豫园老路85号; 6 dumplings upstairs from ¥25, set menu ¥60; ⏰10am-9pm; Ⓜ Yuyuan Garden)

Songyuelou
CHINESE $

6 🍴 Map p52, C2

Shanghai's oldest vegetarian restaurant (dating back to 1910) offers a far more authentic dining experience than most of the tourist-saturated restaurants in the area. English menus upstairs. (松月楼; 99 Jiujiao-chang Rd; 旧校场路99号; dishes ¥25-48; ⏰7am-10pm; 🖊; Ⓜ Yuyuan Garden)

Drinking

Fat Olive
BAR

7 🍷 Map p52, A2

The brainchild of chef David Laris, the Fat Olive serves Greek-style mezze accompanied by a good selection of New World wines. It's nestled among office towers with a cosy outdoor deck overlooking the Old Town. Enter through the Fraser Residence on Shouning Rd. (www.fatolive.com; 6th fl, 228 S Xizang Rd; 西藏南路228号6楼; ⏰11am-1am; 🛜; Ⓜ Dashijie)

Shopping

Dongtai Road Antique Market
ANTIQUES

8 🔒 Map p52, A3

Picking up a genuine antique here is the proverbial needle in a haystack, but there's tremendous variety among the mass-produced Mao memorabilia and other predictable clutter on Dongtai Rd and Liuhekou Rd; haggle hard. (东台路古玩市场; Dongtai Rd; 东台路; ⏰9am-6pm; Ⓜ Laoximen)

Explore

French Concession East

For full immersion in Shanghai's most chic and fashionable charms, there's little need to stray from the French Concession. Once home to the lion's share of Shanghai's adventurers, radicals, gangsters, writers, prostitutes and pimps, Shanghai's very reputation as the 'Paris of the East' evolved from the area's tree-lined streets and European villas.

The Sights in a Day

☀ You can sleep in this morning because not much gets going in the French Concession until 10am at the earliest. Begin the day at **Xintiandi** (p60), where you can explore the Shikumen Open House Museum and stroll the prettified alleyways while boutique hunting. Lunchtime will arrive before you know it, so scout out Xintiandi's fabulous collection of restaurants as you go – **Xinjishi** (p65) and **Crystal Jade** (p65) are two favourites.

☀ Follow the **walking tour** (p108) to get a feel for the Concession's backstreets, shopping strips and historic architecture. Afterwards, head to **Tianzifang** (p58) to check out the Liuli China Museum and assorted galleries before they close for the day, and then it's on to a second round of boutique hopping – or perhaps you'd prefer to celebrate happy hour at the **Alchemist** (p67) or **Kaiba** (p67).

🌙 Evenings are ripe with promise. There's no shortage of great restaurants, such as **Di Shui Dong** (p64) or **Cha's** (p65), which you can follow up with a **massage** (p121) or perhaps a concert at **MAO Livehouse** (p68).

👁 Top Sights

Tianzifang (p58)

Xintiandi (p60)

💗 Best of Shanghai

Eating

Di Shui Dong (p64)

Din Tai Fung (p64)

Cha's (p65)

Crystal Jade (p65)

T8 (p67)

Ye Shanghai (p67)

Boutiques

Tianzifang (p59)

Xintiandi (p68)

Heirloom (p69)

Nine (p69)

PCS (Pop Classic Sneakers; p69)

Huifeng Tea Shop (p69)

Getting There

Ⓜ **Metro** Lines 1 and 10 serve the area, both running east–west past Xintiandi. Line 1 continues on to People's Sq, while line 10 serves the Old Town and E Nanjing Rd (the Bund). The two lines meet at the S Shaanxi Rd metro stop.

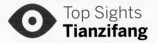

Top Sights
Tianzifang

Xintiandi and Tianzifang (田子坊) are based on a similar idea – an entertainment complex housed within a layout of traditional *longtang* (alleyways) – but when it comes to genuine charm and vibrancy, Tianzifang is the one that delivers. A community of design studios, local families, wi-fi cafes and start-up boutiques, this is the perfect antidote to Shanghai's oversized malls and intimidating skyscrapers.

◉ Map p62, E5

Lane 210, Taikang Rd; 泰康路210弄

ⓂDapuqiao

Exterior of Liuli China Museum

Don't Miss

Shopping

Burrow into the *lilong* (alleys) here for a rewarding haul of creative boutiques, selling everything from hip jewellery and local fashion to retro communist dinnerware. Standout stores include **Shanghai 1936** (Unit 110, No 3, Lane 210) for tailored clothes, **Zhenchalin Tea** (No 13, Lane 210) for herbal tea, **Shokay** (No 9, Lane 274) for silky-soft yak-wool scarves and **Esydragon** (No 20, Lane 210) for souvenirs.

Liuli China Museum

Located across from Tianzifang, this **museum** (琉璃艺术博物馆; www.liulichinamuseum.com; 25 Taikang Rd; admission ¥20; ⏱10am-5pm Tue-Sun) is dedicated to the art of glass sculpture (*pâte de verre* or lost-wax casting). Peruse the collection of ancient Chinese artefacts, contemporary creations and the founders' own sublime Buddhist-inspired pieces. A giant steel peony adorns the building's exterior.

Beaugeste

One of the best galleries in Shanghai, this small **space** (比极影像; www.beaugeste-gallery.com; 5th fl, No 5, Lane 210, Taikang Rd; ⏱10am-6pm) is concealed high above the street-level crowds. Curator Jean Loh focuses on humanistic themes in contemporary Chinese photography, and his wide range of contacts and excellent eye ensure exhibits that are always both moving and thought provoking.

Bars & Cafes

There are several great bars and cafes hidden in the alleyways here, but you may have to spend some time looking for the best places. Top picks include Kommune and Kaiba (p67).

☑ **Top Tips**

▸ Tianzifang consists of three main north–south lanes (Nos 210, 248 and 274) criss-crossed by irregular east–west alleyways, which makes exploration slightly disorienting and fun. Some addresses use Middle Jianguo Rd, which runs parallel to Taikang Rd and serves as the north entrance.

▸ Shops here are generally open from 10am to 8pm.

▸ Although there are plenty of dining options here, there is no Chinese cuisine. You'll most likely have to decide between cafe fare, Thai and pizza.

✕ **Take a Break**

The original Tianzifang cafe, **Kommune** (公社; No 7, Lane 210; meals from ¥58; ⏱7am-1am; 📶) is a consistently bustling hangout with outdoor seating, big breakfasts, sandwiches and barbecue on the menu.

Top Sights
Xintiandi

Xintiandi (新天地) has only been around for a decade and already it's a Shanghai icon. An upscale entertainment complex modelled on traditional *longtang* homes, this was the first development in the city to prove that historic architecture does, in fact, have economic value. Elsewhere that might sound like a no-brainer, but in 21st-century China, which is head-over-heels for the bulldozer, it came as quite a revelation.

◉ Map p62, F2

www.xintiandi.com

2 blocks enclosed within Taicang, Zizhong, Madang & S Huangpi Rds

Ⓜ S Huangpi Rd or Xintiandi

Display at Shikumen Open House Museum

Don't Miss

Shikumen Open House Museum

This invitingly arranged and restored two-storey **stone-gate house** (石库门屋里厢; Xintiandi North Block, No 25; admission ¥20; ⏱10.30am-10.30pm) is decorated with period furniture and infused with the charms of yesteryear Shanghai. Peek into the minute, wedge-shaped *tingzijian* room on the landing, which used to be rented out to cash-strapped writers and other penurious tenants.

Dining

The drinking and dining venues are wedged in cheek by jowl and are what make Xintiandi tick. You can find plenty of coffee and comfort food if that's what you're after, but don't overlook the superb Shanghainese options such as Xinjishi (p65) and Ye Shanghai (p67). For dumplings and dim sum, head to Din Tai Fung (p64) or Crystal Jade (p65).

Shopping

Window shoppers can make a fun afternoon of it here. See p68 for selected stores.

Site of the 1st National Congress of the CCP

The communist narcissism and back-slapping might be irritating to some people, but this lovely *shikumen* **house** (中共一大会址纪念馆; Xintiandi North Block, 76 Xingye Rd; admission free; ⏱9am-5pm, last entry 4pm) is immortalised as one of China's holiest political shrines, where the Chinese Communist Party (CCP) was founded on 23 July 1921. Bring your passport.

☑ Top Tips

▶ The complex is divided into a North Block and a South Block. The North Block is where most of the action is; the South Block is less appealing but has some notable shopping and dining options in the two malls at its southern end.

▶ The **Shanghai Information Centre for International Visitors** (⏱10am-10pm) is located on Xingye Rd at the start of the South Block. You can pick up maps of Xintiandi and Shanghai here, as well as other useful pamphlets.

✕ Take a Break

A place to visit as much for the decor as for the drinks, **TMSK** (透明思考; Xintiandi North Block, Bldg 11; ⏱11.30am-1am) is designed to within an inch of its life; swirled iridescent glass sets the dazzling super-cool ambience.

Shanghai Exhibition Centre

Middle Yan'an Rd 延安中路

Julu Rd 巨鹿路

S Shaanxi Rd 陕西南路

S Maoming Rd

Jinxian Rd

6
3

Ruijin No 1 Rd 瑞金一路

Changle Rd

Jinjiang Tower

N Xiangyang Rd 襄阳北路

Changle Rd

16
Xinle Rd

Xiangyang Park

淮海中路

18
17

Nanchang Rd

5

Donghu Rd

Ruijin No 2 Rd 瑞金二路

S Shaanxi Rd

陕西南路站

13

19

Gaolan Rd 皋兰路

Sun Yatsen's Former Residence

1

20

Xiangshan Rd

复兴中路

Middle Huaihai Rd

Middle Fuxing Rd

12

Fenyang Rd 汾阳路

Middle Fuxing Rd

S Xiangyang Rd

S Shaanxi Rd

S Maoming Rd

Ruijin Hospital

Taiyuan Rd

Yongjia Rd 永嘉路

陕西南路

Shaoxing Rd 绍兴路

11

0   500 m
0   0.25 miles

Middle Jianguo Rd

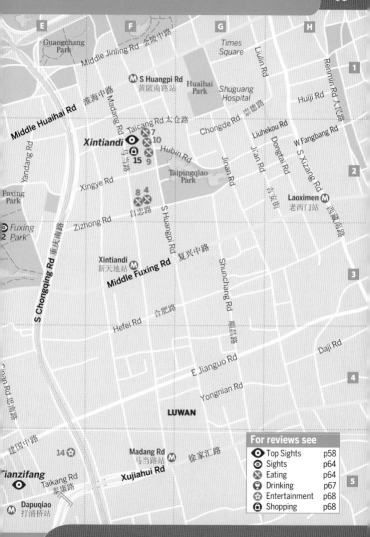

E Guangchang Park

Middle Jinling Rd 金陵中路

Times Square

Liulin Rd

Renmin Rd 人民路

Ⓜ S Huangpi Rd
黄陂南路站

Huaihai Park

Shuguang Hospital

Huiji Rd

淮海中路 Madang Rd

Middle Huaihai Rd

Taicang Rd 太仓路

Chongde Rd 崇德路

Liuhekou Rd

W Fangbang Rd

Yandang Rd

Xintiandi 🅾

⊗ 7

⊗ 10

Jian Rd

Dongtai Rd

S Xizang Rd

🄐
15 9

Hubin Rd

兴业路

Jinan Rd

吉安街

Laoximen
老西门站 Ⓜ

Fuxing Park

Xingye Rd

Taipingqiao Park

西藏南路

🄐 Fuxing
2 Park

8 4
⊗⊗
自忠路

Zizhong Rd

S Huangpi Rd

Xintiandi
新天地站 Ⓜ

复兴中路

Shunchang Rd

S Chongqing Rd 重庆南路

Middle Fuxing Rd

Hefei Rd 合肥路

E Jianguo Rd

Daji Rd

Yongnian Rd

LUWAN

建国中路

14 ✪

Madang Rd
马当路站 Ⓜ

徐家汇路

Tianzifang 🄾

Taikang Rd
泰康路

Xujiahui Rd

思南路

Dapuqiao
打浦桥站 Ⓜ

For reviews see	
🅾 Top Sights	p58
🄾 Sights	p64
⊗ Eating	p64
🄐 Drinking	p67
✪ Entertainment	p68
🄐 Shopping	p68

Sights

Sun Yatsen's Former Residence
HISTORIC RESIDENCE

1 ◉ Map p62, D3

Sun Yatsen (1866–1925), the father of modern China, dwelled in this two-storey house on Rue Molière from 1918 to 1924. It's a simple and retiring slice of Sun Yatsen nostalgia and memorabilia. (孙中山故居; 7 Xiangshan Rd; 香山路7号; admission ¥20; ◷9am-4pm; Ⓜ S Shaanxi Rd or Xintiandi)

Understand

Shanghai's Communist Vestiges

In its bid to totally refashion itself as a global financial centre, Shanghai is deeply at odds with its communist heritage. But lest we forget, the city played a decisive role in China's communist history. China's proletarian destiny was first forged at the Site of the 1st National Congress of the CCP (p61), before the revolution shifted from factory workers to the peasants, and the Gang of Four, who controlled the latter stages of the Cultural Revolution, were based in Shanghai. Other sights include the former residence of Mao Zedong (p89) and the Propaganda Poster Art Centre (p75).

Fuxing Park
PARK

2 ◉ Map p62, E3

Laid out by the French in 1909, this lovely, leafy park is one of the city's most pleasant. There's always plenty to see, whether it be slow-motion taichi types or chess players hunched over their boards in the shade of towering *wutong* trees. (复兴公园; admission free; ◷5am-6pm; Ⓜ S Shaanxi Rd or Xintiandi)

Eating

Di Shui Dong
HUNANESE $$

3 ✕ Map p62, B2

Named after a cave at Mao Zedong's birthplace, this Hunanese eatery's low-key rustic charms are matched by a spicy menu. The claim to fame is the *ziran* (cumin) ribs, but don't miss out on winners such as spicy bean curd or 'Stewed Pork in Sauce of Chairman Mao's Style'. (滴水洞; ☎6253 2689; 2nd fl, 56 S Maoming Rd; 茂名南路 56号2楼; dishes ¥25-88; ◷11am-12.30am; Ⓜ S Shaanxi Rd)

Din Tai Fung
DUMPLINGS $$

4 ✕ Map p62, F2

To-die-for dumplings from Taiwan's most famous chain (p53). It's on the 2nd floor, in the mall. Reserve. (鼎泰丰; ☎6385 8378; Xintiandi South Block, 2nd fl, Bldg 6; 新天地南里6号楼2楼; dumplings ¥58-88; ◷10am-midnight; ✐; Ⓜ S Shaanxi Rd or Xintiandi)

ART ON FILE/ART ON FILE/CORBIS ©

Fuxing Park

Cha's
CANTONESE $

5 Map p62, D2

This absolutely packed Cantonese diner does its best to teleport you to 1950s Hong Kong, with old-style tiled floors, whirring ceiling fans and even an antique Coca-Cola ice box to set the scene. You'll need to wait to get a table, so use the time wisely and peruse the menu in advance. (查餐厅; 30 Sinan Rd; 思南路30号; dishes ¥20-50; ⏱11am-2am; Ⓜ S Shaanxi Rd)

Southern Barbarian
YUNNANESE $$

6 Map p62, B2

Fine, MSG-free Yunnanese cuisine served in a laid-back (though somewhat noisy) atmosphere. Unusual

dishes include the stewed beef and mint casserole, 'grandmother's mashed potatoes' and the addictive chicken wings. Reserve. (南蛮子; ☑5510; 2nd fl, Gourmet Zone, 56 S Maoming Rd; 茂名南路56号生活艺术空间2楼; dishes ¥25-68; Ⓜ S Shaanxi Rd)

Xinjishi
SHANGHAINESE $$

7 Map p62, F2

Branch of classic Shanghainese restaurant Jesse (p77). (新吉士; ☑6336 4746; Bldg 9, Xintiandi North Block; 新天地北里9号楼; dishes ¥38-88; Ⓜ Huangpi Rd or Xintiandi)

Crystal Jade
DIM SUM $$

8 Map p62, F2

What distinguishes Crystal Jade from other dim-sum restaurants is the

Understand

Green Gang Gangsters

In Shanghai's climate of hedonist freedoms, political ambiguities and capitalist free-for-all, it was perhaps inevitable that the city should spawn China's most powerful mobsters. Ironically, in 1930s Shanghai the most binding laws were those of the underworld, with their blood oaths, secret signals and strict code of honour. China's modern-day Triads and Snakeheads owe much of their form to their Shanghainese predecessors.

The real godfather of the Shanghai underworld was Du Yuesheng, or 'Big-Eared' Du as he was known to anyone brave enough to say it to his face. Born in Pudong, Du soon moved across the river and was recruited into the Green Gang (青帮), where he worked for 'Pockmarked' Huang, a legendary gangster who doubled as a high-ranking detective in the French Concession police. Du gained fame by setting up an early opium cartel with the rival Red Gang, and rose through the ranks. By 1927 Du was the head of the Green Gang and in control of the city's prostitution, drug-running, protection and labour rackets. Du's special forte was to kidnap the rich and then to negotiate their release, taking half of the ransom money as commission. With an estimated 20,000 men at his beck and call, Du travelled everywhere in a bullet-proof sedan, protected by armed bodyguards crouched on the running boards.

His control of the labour rackets led to contacts with warlords and politicians. In 1927 Du played a major part in Chiang Kaishek's anti-communist massacre and later became adviser to the Kuomintang. A fervent nationalist, his money supplied the anti-Japanese resistance movement.

Yet Du always seemed to crave respectability. In 1931 he was elected to the Municipal Council and was known for years as the unofficial mayor of Shanghai. He became a Christian halfway through his life and somehow ended up best known as a philanthropist. When the British poet WH Auden visited Shanghai in 1937, Du was head of the Chinese Red Cross!

During the Japanese occupation of Shanghai, Du fled to the city of Chongqing (Chungking). After the war he settled in Hong Kong, where he died, a multimillionaire, in 1951.

dough: dumpling skins are perfectly tender, steamed buns come out light and airy, and the noodles are freshly made. Come for lunch; reservations are recommended. (翡翠酒家; ☑6385 8752; Xintiandi South Block, 2nd fl, Bldg 6, in the mall; 新天地南里6号楼2楼; dim sum dishes ¥16-24; ◷10.30am-11pm; Ⓜ S Huangpi Rd or Xintiandi)

T8
FUSION $$$

 9 Map p62, F2

The seductive grey-brick interior is the perfect setting for the delectable 'Mediterranean with Asian accents' menu (Sichuan high pie, tataki of sesame-crusted tuna), taking diners and Shanghai celebs to new levels of irresistibility. Reserve. (☑6355 8999; Xintiandi North Block, Bldg 8; 太仓路181弄新天地北里8号楼; mains ¥248-598; ◷closed lunch Mon; Ⓜ S Huangpi Rd or Xintiandi)

Ye Shanghai
SHANGHAINESE $$

10 Map p62, F2

Ye offers sophisticated, unchallenging Shanghainese cuisine in classy 1930s-style surroundings. The drunken chicken and smoked fish are an excellent overture to mouth-watering main dishes, such as the crispy duck with pancakes. Reserve. (夜上海; ☑6311 2323; Xintiandi North Block, 338 S Huangpi Rd; 黄陂南路338号新天地北里; dishes ¥38-88; Ⓜ S Huangpi Rd or Xintiandi)

Drinking

Kaiba
BAR

11 Map p62, D5

The Kaiba beer specialists run one of Tianzifang's most popular bars. You'll need to explore to find it. (开巴; www.kaiba-beerbar.com; Tianzifang, 2nd fl, 169 Middle Jianguo Rd; 建国中路169号2楼田子坊; ◷11am-2am; ⊙; Ⓜ Dapuqiao)

Alchemist
BAR

12 Map p62, D3

Molecular is the name of the game here, from the truffled oxtail sliders and curry frites to the magically imbued cocktails that look like they were concocted in the Hogwarts School of Cuisine. (www.alchemistbar.cn; Bldg 32, Sinan Mansions, 45 Sinan Rd; 思南路45号思南公馆32号楼; ◷5pm-2am; Ⓜ Xintiandi)

REDFERNS/GETTY IMAGES ©

Performance by Hanggai at MAO Livehouse

Lou Shi

CAFE

13 Map p62, C3

An antique store–cafe, this homey space is cluttered with Shanghai antiques of every conceivable nature, from the chairs you sit in to stone bodhisattvas, art deco light fixtures and even waffle irons. (陋室; 145 Nanchang Rd; 南昌路145号; ⏰10am-11pm; 📶; Ⓜ S Shaanxi Rd)

Entertainment

MAO Livehouse

LIVE MUSIC

14 ⭐ Map p62, E5

One of the city's best and largest music venues, MAO is a stalwart of the Shanghai music scene, with acts ranging from rock to pop to electronica. (www.mao-music.com; 3rd fl, 308 S Chongqing Rd; 重庆南路308号3楼; Ⓜ Madang Rd)

Shopping

Xintiandi

FASHION, SOUVENIRS

15 🔒 Map p62, F2

The North Block features embroidered accessories at **Annabel Lee** (Bldg 3), high-end fashion from **Shanghai Tang** (Bldg 15) and mod jewellery from **NoD** (Bldg 25). Serious fashionistas should head to the mall **Xintiandi Style** (新天地时尚; 245 Madang Rd; 马当路245号), south of the South Block, which features a good selection of local designers. (新天地; cnr Taicang & Madang

Rds; 太仓路与马当路路口; ⏱11am-11pm;
Ⓜ S Huangpi Rd or Xintiandi)

Heirloom ACCESSORIES

16 🔒 Map p62, A2

Founded in 2008 by two Asian American designers, Heirloom specialises in a range of bold, stylish clutches, satchels and shoulder bags, as well as smaller accessories such as leather wallets and bracelets. Prices range from ¥190 to around ¥4000. (78 Xinle Rd; 新乐路78号; ⏱10.30am-10.30pm; Ⓜ S Shaanxi Rd)

Nine JEWELLERY

17 🔒 Map p62, D2

Drop by this incense-filled boutique to peruse the collection of handmade Tibetan-themed jewellery, fashioned from mother-of-pearl, red coral and turquoise. (142 Nanchang Rd; 南昌路142号; Ⓜ S Shaanxi Rd)

PCS (Pop Classic Sneakers) SHOES

18 🔒 Map p62, D2

This tiny shoebox of a store has a fantastic collection of men's canvas sneakers, all sold at unbeatable prices. Try on a pair of original Feiyue, Warrior or spruced-up Ospop worker boots; owner Jacob Wang will doubtless find the style that suits you best. (130 Nanchang Rd; 南昌路130号; ⏱1-10pm; Ⓜ S Shaanxi Rd)

Heping Finery FASHION

19 🔒 Map p62, C3

S Maoming Rd and Changle Rd are thick with small tailors where you can get sleeved in a *qipao* (cheongsam); this shop offers good value. Tailor-made *qipao* take three to 10 days to make. (和平旗袍专卖店; 161 S Maoming Rd; 茂名南路161号; ⏱9.30am-9.30pm; Ⓜ S Shaanxi Rd)

Huifeng Tea Shop TEA

20 🔒 Map p62, C3

A friendly, reliable tea shop, which has good-quality clay teapots, cups and a great range of Chinese tea. Sample varieties and make your choice, or try 50g of Iron Guanyin (铁观音). (汇丰茶庄; 124 S Maoming Rd; 茂名南路124号; ⏱9am-9.30pm; Ⓜ S Shaanxi Rd)

Explore

French Concession West

The French Concession's western half is an elegant treasure trove of art deco architecture, concession-era villas and atmospheric back-streets. As with the eastern half, shopping, drinking and dining are a visitor's most natural inclinations here. The district is not strong on individual sights, but its attractive streetscapes and inviting tempo make it one of the most stimulating parts of town.

The Sights in a Day

Like the eastern half of the French Concession, the west is a late sleeper, so there's no need to get an early start to the day. Two sights that are open in the morning include the **Propaganda Poster Art Centre** (p75) and the **Shanghai Museum of Arts & Crafts** (p75). Lunch is a short taxi ride away: **Tsui Wah** (p77) and **Baoluo Jiulou** (p77) are two of many options on Fumin Rd.

The numerous boutiques nearby – such as **Yu** (p80) and **NuoMi** (p79) – will keep you dallying in the neighbourhood after you finish your meal, but don't wait too long to explore the **concession-era architecture** (p72) along Wukang Rd.

Dinner will be a tough call. Classy Sichuanese at **Pinchuan** (p76)? Sushi and maki rolls at **Haiku** (p75)? **Yin's** (p75) jazzy decor and superb cuisine might give it the edge if you're feeling romantic. This part of town is where the night owls congregate, so regardless of what comes next, you're in the right place to kick off the evening.

Local Life

Concession-Era Architecture (p72)

Best of Shanghai

Eating

Yin (p75)

Jesse (p77)

Fu 1039 (p76)

Baoluo Jiulou (p77)

Bai's Restaurant (p77)

Drinking

Abbey Road (p78)

el Cóctel (p78)

Apartment (p78)

Cotton's (p78)

Shelter (p78)

Shanghai Brewery (p79)

Fennel (p79)

Getting There

M Metro The western half of the French Concession is served by lines 1, 7 and 10. Line 10 follows Huaihai Rd east–west. Line 1 also follows Huaihai Rd east–west before veering southwest to follow Hengshan Rd. Line 7 connects the French Concession with Jing'an to the north, meeting up with line 1 at the Changshu Rd station.

◯ Local Life
Concession-Era Architecture

The western part of the French Concession was once one of the most desirable addresses in Shanghai, evident from the large and extravagant mansions scattered throughout the area. Although some of these residences are still inhabited, others have been transformed into stylish restaurants, shops, galleries and historic sites, particularly along the century-old Rte Ferguson (today's Wukang Rd).

❶ Yongfoo Elite

Although this 1930s **residence** (雍福会; www.yongfooelite.com; 200 Yongfu Rd; ⏱11.30am-midnight) was once members-only, it's since opened to the general public – great news, because the decor is absolutely stunning. Take time out for afternoon tea or return later for dinner and drinks to fully appreciate the antique-strewn setting, which includes a gorgeous carved archway from Zhejiang in the garden.

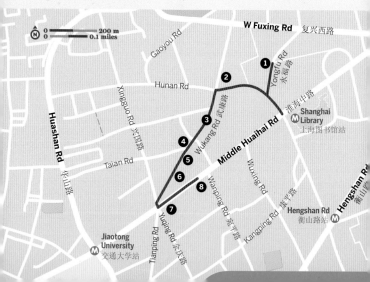

❷ Ba Jin's Former Residence

This French Concession **house** (巴金故居; 113 Wukang Rd; admission free; ◷10am-3pm Tue-Sat) is where the acclaimed writer Ba Jin (1904–2005), author of *Family*, lived from 1955 to the mid-1990s. It contains a small collection of old photos, books and manuscripts. Your passport may be needed for entry.

❸ Route Ferguson

Lined with extravagant villas, Wukang Rd (originally Rte Ferguson) has been a coveted address among Shanghai's movers and shakers ever since its inception in 1907. Generals, mayors, business tycoons and celebrities have lived in these homes since the early 20th century, and there remain over 20 notable heritage buildings along its length.

❹ Leo Gallery

Drop into the red-brick Ferguson Lane complex – a haven for sun-starved diners in nice weather – for a quick tour through the **Leo Gallery** (狮语画廊; 376 Wukang Rd; ◷11am-7pm), which has a rotating line-up of contemporary Chinese art exhibitions. The gallery has a second showroom inside the courtyard.

❺ Wukang Road Tourist Centre

This useful **centre** (武康路旅游咨询中心; 393 Wukang Rd; ◷9am-5pm) displays scale-model concession buildings, photos of historic Shanghai architecture and maps of heritage buildings along Wukang Rd. It's housed in

the former residence of Huang Xing (1874–1916), a revolutionary who cofounded the Republic of China together with Sun Yatsen.

❻ Boutique Break

Don't pass by tiny **Lan Diao** (岚调; 411 Wukang Rd; ◷11am-9pm), which has a charming selection of handicrafts from Guizhou province in southwest China. You'll find shoes, silver jewellery, paper cuts and embroidered fabric, all fashioned by the Miao people, alongside other finds such as paintings and contemporary Chinese-style clothing.

❼ Song Qingling's Former Residence

Built in the 1920s by a Greek shipping magnate, this **building** (宋庆龄故居; 1843 Middle Huaihai Rd; admission ¥20; ◷9am-4.30pm) became home to the wife of Sun Yatsen from 1948 to 1963 and still contains some of her original possessions. It stands across from the landmark Normandie Apartments (1924), whose covered arcade wraps around the intersection of Wukang and Huaihai Rds.

❽ Shanghai Guqin Cultural Foundation

This **cultural centre** (上海古琴文化会; 1801 Middle Huaihai Rd; ◷9am-5pm) offers classes in a handful of traditional arts: Chinese ink painting, *weiqi* (go) and the *guqin* (seven-string zither). Drop by to visit the peaceful 1930s villa and garden and the students might give you a brief demonstration.

For reviews see
- ⊙ Sights — p75
- ⊗ Eating — p75
- ⊕ Drinking — p78
- ★ Entertainment — p79
- 🔒 Shopping — p79

Wanhangdu Rd 万航渡路

Jing'an Temple 静安寺站

W Nanjing Rd 南京西路

Shanghai Exhibition Centre

Jiangsu Rd 江苏路站

Zhenning Rd 镇宁路

Yuyuan Rd 愚园路

Jing'an Park

Middle Yan'an Rd 延安中路

Julu Rd 巨鹿路

25

Jiangsu Rd 江苏路

Dong Zhu'anbang Rd 东诸安浜路

17

W Yan'an Rd 延安西路

Fumin Rd 富民路

Xinle Rd

Donghu Rd

10 15 26 22 9 8 20

Huashan Rd 华山路

Changle Rd 长乐路

Changshu Rd 常熟路

Huaihai Rd

Propaganda Poster Art Centre 1

Anfu Rd

S Wulumuqi Rd 五原路

S Wulumuqi Rd 乌鲁木齐

Middle Huaihai Rd 淮海中路

Changshu Rd 常熟路站

Caojiayan Rd 曹家堰路

23

24

Baoqing Rd 宝庆路

21

Middle Fuxing Rd 复兴中路

Ding Xiang Garden

Wuyuan Rd 五原路

12 14 19 18

W Fuxing Rd 复兴西路

Shanghai Museum of Arts & Crafts 3

Gaoyou Rd

27

Yongfu Rd 永福路

Taojiang Rd

Dongping Rd 东平路

7 5 16

Huashan Rd

Xinguo Rd 新国路

Wukang Rd

Middle Huaihai Rd

Shanghai Library 上海图书馆站

4

S Wulumuqi Rd 乌鲁木齐南路

Yongjia Rd 永嘉路

Yueyang Rd 岳阳路

Taiyuan Rd 太原路

11

W Jianguo Rd 建国西路

Fahuazhen Rd 法华镇路

Jiaotong University 交通大学站

Taian Rd

Tianping Rd

Hengshan Rd 衡山路

Wuxing Rd

Hengshan Rd 衡山路站

Anting Rd

W Huaihai Rd 淮海西路

Jiaotong University

Kangping Rd

Wanping Rd

Hengshan Rd

13

2 CY Tung Maritime Museum

Sights

Propaganda Poster Art Centre
GALLERY

1 ◎ Map p74, B3

With the Cultural Revolution still a no-go zone for aspiring intellectuals and journalists, Shanghai distils the cream of its Communist propaganda at this fascinating basement museum and shop, where 3000 posters from Mao's heyday broadcast their unwavering message of utopian bliss. Look out for the big character posters *(dazibao),* a rare and vanishing breed. (宣传画黏画艺术中心; ☑ 6211 1845; www.shanghaipropagandaart.com; Room B-OC, President Mansion, 868 Huashan Rd; 华山路868号; admission ¥20; ⊙ 10am-4.30pm; Ⓜ Shanghai Library)

CY Tung Maritime Museum
MUSEUM

2 ◎ Map p74, A5

This small museum explores the little-known world of Chinese maritime history, with model ships, maps of early trade routes and exhibits on the legendary Chinese Muslim seafarer Zheng He and the maritime Silk Route. (董浩云航运博物馆; Jiaotong University, 1954 Huashan Rd; 华山路1954号交通大学内; admission free; ⊙ 1.30-5.30pm Tue-Sun; Ⓜ Jiaotong University)

Shanghai Museum of Arts & Crafts
MUSEUM

3 ◎ Map p74, D4

Catch crafts emerging from the skilled fingers of on-site artisans, watch Chinese paper-cutting, embroidery and lacquer work and get your souvenir shopping sorted. The lovely building (built in 1905) and its gorgeous lawn are showpiece extras. (上海工艺美术博物馆; 79 Fenyang Rd; 汾阳路79号; admission ¥8; ⊙ 9am-4pm; Ⓜ Changshu Rd)

Eating

Yin
CHINESE $$$

4 🍴 Map p74, C4

A throwback to the 1930s, Yin emanates soft, jazzy decadence with its antique furnishings, Song-dynasty-style tableware and Ella Fitzgerald on the stereo. But here they're as much visionaries as they are traditionalists. The kitchen has adopted older cooking techniques – back from the days before MSG – and prepares standout regional dishes from across China, including the superbly named 'squid lost in a sandstorm'. (音; ☑ 5466 5070; 2nd fl, 4 Hengshan Rd; 衡山路4号2楼; dishes ¥38-108; Ⓜ Hengshan Rd)

Haiku
JAPANESE $$$

5 🍴 Map p74, D4

The wackiest maki rolls in town: try out the Ninja (shrimp, crab and a killer spicy sauce), the Clayton (shiitake mushrooms, snow crab and scorched white tuna), the Sweepee (sweet potatoes, avocado and sesame seeds) or, for the indecisive, Pimp My Roll (everything). Book ahead. (隐泉之语; ☑6445 0021; 28b Taojiang Rd; 桃江路28号乙; maki rolls ¥68-98; 🖊; Ⓜ Changshu Rd)

Fu 1039   SHANGHAINESE $$$

6 🍴 Map p74, A2

Set in a three-storey 1913 villa, Fu attains an old-fashioned charm uncommon in design-driven Shanghai. The succulent smoked-fish starter and the stewed pork in soy sauce are recommended, with the sweet-and-sour Mandarin fish coming in close behind. The entrance, down an alley and on the left, is unmarked. Minimum charge of ¥200 per head. Reserve. (福一零三九; ☑5237 1878; 1039 Yuyuan Rd; 愚园路1039号; dishes ¥48-108; Ⓜ Jiangsu Rd)

Pinchuan   SICHUANESE $$$

7 🍴 Map p74, C4

Even though Pinchuan has hit the upscale button repeatedly in the past few years, this revamped villa is still a fine place to experience the peculiar tongue-tingling sensation of Sichuanese cuisine. Try the sliced beef in spicy sauce, baked spare ribs with peanuts, or spicy chicken. Book ahead. (品川; ☑400 820 7706; 47 Taojiang Rd; 桃江路47号; dishes ¥39-90; Ⓜ Changshu Rd)

Artisan at work, Shanghai Museum of Arts & Crafts (p75)

Ⓠ Local Life
Shanghai Flavours

Shanghai cuisine's emphasis on sweetness and seafood is not for everyone, but even the most finicky eater will revel in the home-cooked flavours of long-time favourite **Jesse** (Map p74, B5; 吉士酒楼; ☑6282 9260; 41 Tianping Rd; 天平路41号; dishes ¥28-98; Ⓜ Jiaotong University). The unassuming **Bai's Restaurant** (Map p74, C5; 白家餐室; ☑6437 6915; No 12, Lane 189, Wanping Rd; 宛平路189 弄12号; dishes ¥24-78; Ⓜ Hengshan Rd or Zhaojiabang Rd) is another good choice – the simple dining room is like being invited into someone's home. Reserve for both.

Tsui Wah   CANTONESE $

8 🍴 Map p74, D2

The famous Hong Kong tea restaurant has finally set up shop in Shanghai, garnering instant acclaim not only among homesick Hong Kongers but pretty much everyone else in the 'hood. Notable dishes include Hainan chicken and the Malaysian curries, but the menu skips from Cantonese to Italian pasta without missing a beat. (翠华餐厅; 291 Fumin Rd; 富民路291号; dishes ¥32-68; ⏱11am-1am; Ⓜ Changshu Rd or S Shaanxi Rd)

Noodle Bull   NOODLES $

Far cooler than your average street-corner noodle stand (minimalist concrete chic and funky bowls),

MSG-free Noodle Bull is also flat-out delicious. It doesn't matter whether you go vegetarian or for the roasted-beef noodles, it's hard not to find satisfaction. Around the corner from Tsui Wah (see 8 🍴 Map p74, D2). (狠牛面; ☑6170 1299; Unit 3b, 291 Fumin Rd, entrance on Changle Rd; 富民路291号1F3B室; noodles ¥28-35; ✐; Ⓜ Changshu Rd or S Shaanxi Rd)

Baoluo Jiulou   SHANGHAINESE $$

9 🍴 Map p74, D2

The scorching popularity of this unpretentious venue is a sure sign of good cookin', with much-cherished Shanghai favourites such as lemon-drizzled eel and lion's-head meatballs. (保罗酒楼; ☑6279 2827; 271 Fumin Rd; 富民路271号; dishes ¥20-68; ⏱11am-3am; Ⓜ Changshu Rd or Jing'an Temple)

Pho Real   VIETNAMESE $$

10 🍴 Map p74, B2

This ultra-hip pint-sized eatery, decked out with woven fishing traps suspended from the ceiling and a bright blue-and-white colour scheme, serves what many believe to be the best *pho* (beef noodle soup flavoured with mint, star anise and cilantro) and spring rolls in town. It only seats about 20 and there are no reservations, so show up early and come prepared to wait. (166 Fumin Rd; 富民路166号; noodles ¥48-60; Ⓜ Changshu Rd or Jing'an Temple)

Drinking

Abbey Road
BAR

11 🍷 Map p74, D4

Once the weather gets nice, the tree-shaded patio adds the final ingredient to make this cheap beer and classic rock combination an irresistible favourite. (艾比之路; ☏6431 6787; 45 Yueyang Rd; 岳阳路45号; ⏱4pm-late Mon-Fri, 8.30am-late Sat & Sun; 🛜; Ⓜ Changshu Rd)

el Cóctel
BAR

12 🍷 Map p74, C3

This artsy, retro cocktail lounge mixes up some damn fine drinks, with a mixology list that goes beyond the usual suspects. Reserve. (☏6433 6511; 2nd fl, 47 Yongfu Rd; 永福路47号; ⏱5pm-3am; Ⓜ Shanghai Library)

Apartment
BAR

This trendy loft-style bar next to el Cóctel (see **12** 🍷 Map p74, C3) is designed to appeal to the full spectrum of 30-something professionals, with a surprisingly artsy events program and neighbouring dance space. (3rd fl, 47 Yongfu Rd; 永福路47号; ⏱11am-2am; 🛜; Ⓜ Shanghai Library)

Cotton's
BAR

13 🍷 Map p74, C5

Cotton's French Concession concept – an evocative 1930s villa, restful garden and gorgeous interior – sets

---

Ⓠ Local Life
Shanghai Clubbing

One of the city's most popular party spots, **No 88** (Map p74, D2; 搜浩88酒吧; www.no88bar.com; 2nd fl, 291 Fumin Rd; 富民路291号; ⏱9pm-6am; Ⓜ S Shaanxi Rd or Changshu Rd) is the place to go when you're ready to get down Shanghai style, with over-the-top baroque decor, nonstop drinking games and lots of whisky and green tea.

---

the standard for Shanghai's bars. (棉花酒吧; 132 Anting Rd; 安亭路132号; ⏱11am-2am; 🛜; Ⓜ Hengshan Rd)

Shelter
CLUB

14 🍷 Map p74, C3

The darling of the underground crowd, this reconverted bomb shelter is the city's best spot for serious music (cutting-edge DJs and hip-hop artists) and cheap drinks. (5 Yongfu Rd; 永福路5号; ⏱9pm-4am Wed-Sat; Ⓜ Shanghai Library)

Dr Wine
BAR

15 🍷 Map p74, D2

Black-leather armchairs, salvaged *shikumen* (stone-gate house) brick walls and worn-in tables set the mood at this casual two-storey wine bar. (177 Fumin Rd; 富民路177号; ⏱11am-2am; 🛜; Ⓜ Jing'an Temple)

Shanghai Brewery
BAR

16 🅗 Map p74, C4

Handcrafted microbrews, a huge range of comfort food, pool tables and sports on TV... This massive two-storey hangout might have it all. (15 Dongping Rd; 东平路15号; ⏱10am-2am; 📶; Ⓜ Changshu Rd or Hengshan Rd)

Fennel
BAR

17 🅣 Map p74, B2

This classy cocktail lounge features two cosy seating areas and an eclectic line-up of live acoustic performances (everything from jazz to traditional Chinese music). (回香; 217 Zhenning Rd, entrance on Dong Zhu'anbang Rd; 镇宁路217号; Ⓜ Jiangsu Rd)

Entertainment

Cotton Club
JAZZ

18 ⭐ Map p74, C4

In a space decked out in wood and brass, the longstanding Cotton Club's house band serves up live jazz and blues to a loyal crowd. (棉花俱乐部; 📞6437 7110; 8 W Fuxing Rd; 复兴西路8号; ⏱7.30pm-2am Tue-Sun; Ⓜ Changshu Rd)

JZ Club
JAZZ

19 ⭐ Map p74, C3

This is a clued-up setting where contemporary jazz, Latin and R&B sounds are enjoyed by an enthusiastic following. (📞6385 0269; 46 W Fuxing Rd; 复兴西路46号; ⏱9pm-2am; Ⓜ Changshu Rd)

Shopping

NuoMi
FASHION

20 🔒 Map p74, D2

This Shanghai-based label seems to do everything right: gorgeous dresses made from organic cotton, silk and bamboo, eye-catching jewellery fashioned from recycled materials, a sustainable business plan that gives back to the community and even an irresistible line of kids' clothes. (糯米; www.nuomishanghai.com; 196 Xinle Rd; 新乐路196号; Ⓜ Changshu Rd)

Understand

Seduction & the City

Shanghai owes its reputation as the most fashionable city in China to the calendar poster, whose print runs once numbered in the tens of millions and whose distribution reached from China's interior to Southeast Asia. The basic idea behind the poster was to associate a product with an attractive woman, to encourage subconscious desire and consumption. Not only did calendar posters introduce new products to Chinese everywhere but also their portrayal of Shanghai women – wearing make-up and stylish clothing, smoking cigarettes and surrounded by foreign goods – set the standard for modern fashion that many Chinese women would dream of for decades.

ALEX SEGRE / ALAMY ©

Xinle Rd

XinleLu.com

FASHION

21 🔒 Map p74, C3

Local style mavens XinleLu.com have finally ventured out into the offline world with this original showroom, displaying the best of their hand-picked bags, shoes and dresses from local designers. Also sharing the space is vintage specialist William the Beekeeper. (www.xinlelu.com; 87 Wuyuan Rd; 五原路87号; ⊗noon-10pm Tue-Sun; Ⓜ Changshu Rd)

Yu

CERAMICS

22 🔒 Map p74, D2

Man Zhang and her husband create the personable porcelain at this tiny shop, the latest link in the Shanghai-Jingdezhen connection. It's an excellent place to browse for handmade and hand-painted tea ware, bowls and vases. (英; 164 Fumin Rd; 富民路164号; ⊗11am-9pm; Ⓜ Changshu Rd)

Ba Yan Ka La

BEAUTY

23 🔒 Map p74, B3

This well-conceived store offers a luxurious line of natural beauty products derived from Chinese herbal medicine. Goji berry (skin revitalisation), lotus seed (skin nourishment) and mulberry (detoxification) are the principal ingredients in the shampoos, bath salts, facial scrubs and scented candles. (巴颜喀拉; 1221 Changle Rd; 长乐路1221号; ⊗10am-9pm; Ⓜ Changshu Rd)

Mayumi Sato
FASHION

24 🔒 Map p74, C3

Japanese designer Mayumi Sato uses organic cotton, silk and wool to create a playful collection of limited-edition skirts, dresses and tops. Nothing is mass produced and offcuts are recycled into her line of signature accessories. (169 Anfu Rd; 安福路169号; ⊙noon-8pm; Ⓜ Changshu Rd)

Brocade Country
HANDICRAFTS

25 🔒 Map p74, D2

Peruse an exquisite collection of minority handicrafts from China's southwest, most of which are second-hand (ie not made for the tourist trade) and personally selected by owner Liu Xiaolan, a Guizhou native. (锦绣纺; 616 Julu Rd; 巨鹿路616号; ⊙10am-7.30pm; Ⓜ Changshu Rd or Jing'an Temple)

Madame Mao's Dowry
MEMORABILIA, FASHION

26 🔒 Map p74, D2

The seamless transition from notorious revolutionary to chic mantelpiece ornament took place with hardly a wobble. Bag Mao's bust, a repro revolutionary tin mug or designer clothing and jewellery. (毛太设计; 207 Fumin Rd; 富民路207号; ⊙10am-7pm; Ⓜ Changshu Rd or Jing'an Temple)

Urban Tribe
FASHION

27 🔒 Map p74, C4

This eco-conscious Shanghai label draws inspiration from the ethnic groups of Southeast Asia. Urban Tribe's collection of loose-fitting blouses, pants and jackets are made of natural fabrics; it also designs attractive silver jewellery. (城市山民; 133 W Fuxing Rd; 复兴西路133号; ⊙10am-10pm; Ⓜ Shanghai Library)

Explore

Jing'an

The vibrant commercial district of Jing'an has evolved into a popular business, shopping and residential zone, defined by the pulsing throb of W Nanjing Rd (named Bubbling Well Rd in concession times). Art lovers can forage north to M50, Buddhists will make a beeline for the Jade Buddha Temple, while foodies will have their hands full deciding where to eat.

The Sights in a Day

☼ Jing'an is a fascinating neighbourhood to explore, and there's no better way to do it than on foot. Learn about the **local architecture** (p88) around W Nanjing Rd, where you can visit alleyway housing and one of Mao Zedong's former residences. Stop for an early lunch at **Vegetarian Lifestyle** (p92) or **Wujiang Road Food Street** (p92) and then head to **Jade Buddha Temple** (p84), or visit the temple first followed by lunch at the adjacent vegetarian canteen.

☼ Taxi it over to nearby **M50** (p86), where you can sift through the experiments taking place in the contemporary-art world and get a feel for the issues that preoccupy modern Chinese society. After an energising coffee on the roof of building 17, taxi it over to **Jing'an Temple** (p92; pictured left), where the statuary contrasts markedly with that of Jade Buddha Temple.

☽ For dinner, go sophisticated: classy Hunanese at **Guyi** (p92) or scrumptious Shanghai-Cantonese hybrid **Lynn** (p92), followed by an evening with the acrobats at **Shanghai Centre Theatre** (p93).

◉ Top Sights

Jade Buddha Temple (p84)

M50 (p86)

◯ Local Life

Jing'an Architecture (p88)

♥ Best of Shanghai

Eating

Vegetarian Lifestyle (p92)

Jade Buddha Temple (p85)

Qimin Organic Hotpot (p93)

Ceramics

Spin (p94)

Jingdezhen Porcelain Artware (p89)

Entertainment

Shanghai Centre Theatre (p93)

Bandu Cabin (p93)

Getting There

Ⓜ **Metro** Line 2 runs beneath W Nanjing Rd, stopping at People's Sq, W Nanjing Rd and Jing'an Temple. Line 7 runs from north Jing'an to the French Concession, with handy junctions at Jing'an Temple and Changshou Rd. The new line 13 will link Changshou Rd in north Jing'an with W Nanjing Rd.

Top Sights
Jade Buddha Temple

One of Shanghai's few active Buddhist monasteries, this temple was built between 1918 and 1928. The highlight is a transcendent Buddha made of pure jade, one of five shipped back to China by the monk Hui Gen at the turn of the 20th century, following a pilgrimage from the Buddhist island of Putuoshan to Myanmar (Burma) via Tibet.

◉ Map p90, D2

cnr Anyuan & Jiangning Rds; 安远路和江宁路拐角

admission ¥20

⊙ 8am-4.30pm

🚌 19 from Broadway Mansions along Tiantong Rd

Ⓜ Changshou Rd

Jade Buddha Temple

Don't Miss

Hall of Heavenly Kings

Although you no longer enter through the original entrance hall, this hall – on your right as you come in – should be the first one you visit, with its namesake kings (Growth, Knowledge, the All-Seeing, and Protector of the Country) and a splendid statue of the Laughing Buddha back-to-back with a fabulous effigy of Weituo, the guardian of Buddhism.

Great Treasure Hall

Festooned with red lanterns and paved with slabs etched with lotus flowers, the first courtyard leads to the twin-eaved Great Treasure Hall, where worshippers pray to the past, present and future Buddhas, which are seated on splendidly carved thrones. Also lodged within the main hall are the temple's drum and bell, which would normally be hung within separate towers.

Jade Buddha Hall

Follow the right-hand corridor past the Hall of Heavenly Kings and the Guanyin Hall to arrive at the **Jade Buddha Hall** (separate admission ¥10). The absolute centrepiece of the temple is the 1.9m-high pale-green jade Buddha, which is seated up-stairs. Visitors are not able to approach the statue but can admire it from a distance. Photographs are not permitted.

Ancestral Hall

On your right as you exit the Jade Buddha Hall is the Ancestral Hall, where Buddhist services are held. Turning around and heading back towards the entrance will then take you past a similarly elegant jade **reclining Buddha**, opposite a larger copy made from marble, which originated in Singapore.

☑ Top Tips

▶ In February, during the Lunar New Year, the temple is very busy, as some 20,000 Chinese Buddhists throng here to pray for prosperity.

▶ The surrounding shops and hawkers sell everything you need to generate good fortune, including bundles of spirit money and incense sticks.

▶ Look for statues of Guanyin, the goddess of mercy, throughout the temple. One is located at the rear of the Great Treasure Hall; she also has her own hall on the far side of the first courtyard.

✕ Take a Break

Pull up a seat alongside the monks, nuns and lay worshippers at this two-storey Buddhist **banquet hall** (玉佛寺素斋; 999 Jiangning Rd; 江宁路999号; dishes ¥18-36; ⓜChangshou Rd) for a vegetarian feast.

Top Sights
M50

Chinese contemporary art has been the hottest thing in the art world for over a decade now, and there's no sign of the boom ending, with collectors around the world paying record prices for the work of top artists. Beijing may dominate the art scene, but Shanghai has its own thriving gallery subculture, centred on this complex of industrial buildings (once a textile mill) down dusty Moganshan Rd in the north of town.

👁 Map p90, E1

50 Moganshan Rd; 莫干山路50号

Ⓜ Shanghai Railway Station or taxi

Artwork by Wang Guangyi, ShanghART

Don't Miss

ShanghART

The most established gallery here, the 17-year-old **ShanghArt** (www.shanghartgallery.com; Bldgs 16 & 18) was founded by Swiss-born Lorenz Helbling in 1996. It now has two big, dramatic spaces to show the work of some of the 40 artists it represents, including M50 pioneers Ding Yi and Zhou Tiehai.

island6

The top-notch and provocative **island6** (www.island6.org; 2nd fl, Bldg 6) is an art collective that focuses on collaborative works created in a studio behind the gallery. Known as Liu Dao in Chinese, the studio consists of an international (and rotating) group of artists and techies, and often experiments with media such as LED art, photography and digital works.

m97

Located across the street from M50, **m97** (www.m97gallery.com; 2nd fl, 97 Moganshan Rd) is the largest photography gallery in Shanghai, representing some two-dozen China-based photographers. Expect thought-provoking and excellent-quality exhibits year round, with styles that range from portraits to landscapes to conceptual. The entrance can be tricky to locate.

Other Galleries

Other notable galleries include **Other Gallery** (www.othergallery.com.cn; Bldg 9), which first opened in Beijing in 2009 before setting up in Shanghai, and **twocities** (www.twocitiesgallery.com; 2nd fl, Bldg 0), which features sculpture, generally in glass, ceramics or lacquer, and jewellery. They also host occasional music performances and film screenings. Huang Yunhe's **OFoto** (www.ofoto-gallery.com; 2nd fl, Bldg 13) features contemporary photography exhibitions.

☑ Top Tips

▶ Most galleries are open from 10am to 6pm; the majority close on Monday.

▶ There are a lot of commercial spaces here selling unimaginative, mass-produced artwork. It can be hard to recognise initially, so start with the galleries listed here for the best introduction. As a general rule, you can skip buildings 3 and 4 near the entrance.

✗ Take a Break

In nice weather, the best place to pull up a seat is the **Roof Club** (rooftop, Bldg 17; ⊙11am-7pm), where you can get tea, coffee and snacks served up with appropriately industrial views. Alternatively, break for a bowl of noodles at Bandu Cabin (p93).

Local Life
Jing'an Architecture

Jing'an boasts an unusual melange of architectural styles, ranging from Shanghai-style row housing and 1920s apartment blocks to Christian and Jewish temples of worship. One of the greatest concentrations of old buildings can be found on N Shaanxi Rd (formerly Seymour Rd). For a snapshot of everyday Shanghai life, this is a great place to start.

❶ Bubbling Well Road Apartments

One of the most delightful surviving new-style *lilong* (alley) housing complexes in Shanghai, Bubbling Well Road Apartments (静安别墅) consists of three-storey red-brick houses built between 1928 and 1932. It's a great spot to observe daily residential life and explore a new crop of tiny ground-floor cafes and boutiques.

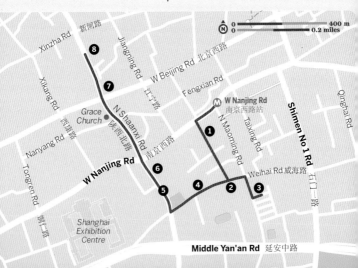

❷ Sun Court

Across the street from Bubbling Well is **Sun Court** (651 Weihai Rd), a multi-storey apartment building completed in 1928. Although it was named after real estate mogul Sun Chunsheng (1899–1974), the Chinese translator mistakenly used 太阳 ('sun' in the sky) instead of 孙 (Sun's name) when assigning the Chinese name. Peek into the leafy inner courtyard.

❸ Mao Zedong's Former Residence

Mao lived **here** (毛泽东旧居; Nos 5-9, 120 N Maoming Rd; 茂名北路120弄5-9号; admission free; ☺9-11am & 1-4pm; Ⓜ W Nanjing Rd) in the latter half of 1924 with his second wife, Yang Kaihui, and their two children. The residence is a beautiful example of *shikumen* (stone-gate house) architecture. Passport required for entry.

❹ Tea Shop

The **Xiao Ye Tea Shop** (小叶名茶; 686 Weihai Rd; ☺7.30am-9.30pm) has a good collection of *pu'erh* (aged fermented tea from Yunnan) cakes and bricks lining the walls, as well as loose-leaf oolong, white and herbal teas for sale. The back room also sells teapots and utensils.

❺ North Shaanxi Road

The garden residence (1918) at No 186 once belonged to Wuxi native Rong Zongjing, one of Shanghai's most powerful industrialists at the time. Rong Zongjing's nephew, Rong Yiren, was one of the rare individuals with a capitalist background to succeed in communist China, becoming vice mayor of Shanghai in 1957 and later vice president of the country from 1993 to 1998.

❻ Jingdezhen Porcelain Artware

This is one of the best **stores** (景德镇艺术瓷器; 212 N Shaanxi Rd; 陕西北路212号; Ⓜ W Nanjing Rd) for high-quality traditional Chinese porcelain. Blue-and-white vases, plates, teapots and cups are among the many choices. International shipping available.

❼ Sea-Salt Coffee Break

Not far from Grace Baptist Church at No 375 (moved here in 1942) is Taiwanese coffee and tea chain **Café 85°C** (85度C咖啡店; 408 N Shaanxi Rd; ☺24hr; Ⓜ W Nanjing Rd). Drop in for quality, inexpensive coffee (including sea-salt coffee) and tea, and why not pick up a few of those unusual pastries while you're at it?

❽ Ohel Rachel Synagogue

This **synagogue** (500 N Shaanxi Rd) was built by Jacob Sassoon in 1920, and was the first of seven synagogues built in Shanghai (only two remain). It was constructed in the Greek Revival style, inspired by the Sephardic synagogues of London, such as Bevis Marks. It is unfortunately closed to the public.

E · F · G · H

M50

Shànghǎi Railway Station M
上海火车站

Moganshan Rd 莫干山路

W Tianmu Rd 天目西路

Meiyuan Rd

Middle Tianmu Rd

Gonghexin Rd

Haining Rd 海宁路

Chang'an Rd

Yutong Rd

Hengfeng Rd

Minli Rd

Hanzhong Rd 汉中路

Hengtong Rd

Datong Rd 大统路

Wuzhen Rd 乌镇路

Jinyuan Rd 晋元路

Wusong River (Suzhou Creek)

Haifang Rd

Hanzhong Rd
汉中路站

Guangfu Rd 光复路

Datian Rd 大田路

S Suzhou Rd 南苏州路

Xinzha Rd
新闸路站

Xinzha Rd 新闸路

Changping Rd

Jiangning Rd

Moganshan Rd

Shanhaiguan Rd 山海关路

Shimen No 2 Rd 石门二路

W Beijing Rd 北京西路

Huanghe Rd 黄河路

10

Wuding Rd 武定路

Xinzha Rd 新闸路

Fengyang Rd 凤阳路

Xinchang

Xikang Rd 西康路

W Beijing Rd 北京西路

Fengxian Rd

Wujiang Rd 吴江路

N Chengdu Rd 成都北路

11

Jiangyin Rd

N Huangpi Rd 黄陂北路

5

2

W Nanjing Rd

Shimen No 1 Rd 石门一路

Qinghai Rd 青海路

Sanjiao Park

Fengxian Rd

7
Nanyang Rd

3

6

W Nanjing Rd
南京西路站

Westgate Mall

Weihai Rd 威海路

N Maoming Rd

Wusheng Rd 武胜路

Tongren Rd 铜仁路

8

N Shaanxi Rd

Dagu Rd

W Nanjing Rd
南京西路

Shanghai Exhibition Centre

Dagu Rd

S Chengdu Rd

Guang'ehang Park

Changde Rd 常德路

S Shaanxi Rd 陕西南路

Ruijin No 1 Rd
瑞金一路

Changle Rd

Middle Yan'an Rd
中山中路 延安中路

S Maoming Rd

1

2

3

4

5

N 500 m · 0.25 miles

Sights

Jing'an Temple

TEMPLE

1 📍 Map p90, D5

After over a decade of restoration, Jing'an Temple is finally coming together as one of the city's most eye-catching temples. Although it lacks an air of venerability and there are fewer devotees than at the Jade Buddha Temple (p84), there can be no denying its spectacular location among the district's soaring skyscrapers or the impressive statuary inside. (静安寺; 1686-1688 W Nanjing Rd; 南京西路1686-1688号; admission ¥30; ⏱7.30am-5pm; Ⓜ Jing'an Temple)

Eating

Vegetarian Lifestyle

CHINESE, VEGETARIAN $$

2 🍴 Map p90, F4

The Chinese sign on the door says it all: 'No smoking, no alcohol, no eggs and no meat'. The food here is simply delectable, and the health-conscious, ecofriendly mentality extends all the way to the toothpicks (made from cornflour). (枣子树; 258 Fengxian Rd; 奉贤路258号; dishes ¥22-68; ⏱11am-9pm; 🖋; Ⓜ W Nanjing Rd)

Lynn

SHANGHAINESE $$$

3 🍴 Map p90, E4

Newfangled dim sum and Shanghai-meets-Cantonese cuisine in a splendidly stylish setting. Adventurous standouts mix with traditional dishes: look for eggplant with minced pork, chicken with sesame pockets and deep-fried ribs with honey and garlic. Sunday brings an all-you-can-eat brunch. Reserve. (琳怡; 📞6247 0101; 99-1 Xikang Rd; 西康路99-1号; dishes ¥48-125; ⏱11.30am-10.30pm; Ⓜ W Nanjing Rd)

Guyi Hunan Restaurant

HUNANESE $$

4 🍴 Map p90, D5

Crowd into the lift with nearby office workers and ascend to sophisticated Hunanese and mouth-watering cumin ribs right next to Jing'an Temple (it's in the mall). (古意湘味浓; 📞6232 8377;

🔍 Local Life
Wujiang Road Food Street

This pedestrian food street (吴江路休闲街) has still got the goods when it comes to snack food. If you can beat the mealtime rush, the first spot to go scavenging is the multi-storey building at No 269 (above one of the W Nanjing Rd metro exits). The 2nd floor here has two of the city's most famous chains: the **Nanxiang Steamed Bun Restaurant** (p55) and a much-too-small outlet of **Yang's Fry Dumplings** (p38). Down at street level, you'll find plenty of cafes, Japanese ramen chains, ice-cream vendors and stalls selling more traditional snacks such as roasted chestnuts.

8th fl, City Plaza, 1618 W Nanjing Rd; 南京西路1618号8楼久百城市广场; dishes ¥28-98; M Jing'an Temple)

Qimin Organic Hotpot

HOTPOT $$$

5 🍴 Map p90, E4

Qimin makes use of a 6th-century treatise on agriculture and food preparation to prepare healthy, sophisticated hotpots for discerning diners. (齐民有机中国火锅; ☎6258 8777; 407 N Shaanxi Rd; 陕西北路407号; set menu lunch Mon-Fri ¥78-98, set menu dinner ¥178-238; 🖊; M W Nanjing Rd)

Shanghai Centre

VARIOUS $$

The always hopping Shanghai Centre (see 8 ⭐ Map p90, E4) has sublime dumplings from Din Tai Fung (p53), health-conscious cafes Element Fresh and Baker & Spice, and even the city's best thin-crust pizzas from Pizza Marzano. (上海商城; 1376 W Nanjing Rd; 南京西路1376号; 🍽🖊; M Jing'an Temple or W Nanjing Rd)

Drinking

Wagas

CAFE

6 🍷 Map p90, F4

A dependable local cafe that's good for coffee and Western breakfast. Locations throughout Shanghai. (沃歌斯; www.wagas.com.cn; Bldg 11a, Citic Sq, 1168 W Nanjing Rd; 南京西路1168号下一层11a室; ⏰7am-9.30pm; 🛜; M W Nanjing Rd)

Big Bamboo

BAR

7 🍷 Map p90, E4

This is a huge, extroverted sports bar ranging over two floors with a mammoth sports screen backed up by a constellation of TV sets, Guinness, pool and darts. (132 Nanyang Rd; 南阳路132号; ⏰9.30am-2am; 🛜; M Jing'an Temple)

Entertainment

Shanghai Centre Theatre

ACROBATICS

8 ⭐ Map p90, E4

With joint-popping performances at 7.30pm most nights, this is one of the main venues in town for acrobatics. Routines from the Shanghai Acrobatics Troupe rotate nightly, but don't attempt them at home. (上海商城剧院; ☎6279 8948; www.pujiangqing.com; 1376 W Nanjing Rd; 南京西路1376号; tickets ¥100-280; M Jing'an Temple or W Nanjing Rd)

Bandu Cabin

LIVE MUSIC

Phone up after 10am on Friday and book a seat for the traditional Chinese music performances every Saturday at 7.30pm (¥50) at this cafe at the M50 complex (see ◉ Map p90, E1). (半度音乐; ☎6276 8267; www.bandumusic.com; Bldg 11, 50 Moganshan Rd; 莫干山路50号11号楼; ⏰10am-6.30pm Sun-Fri, to 10pm Sat; M Shanghai Railway Station)

KYLIE MCLAUGHLIN/GETTY IMAGES ©

Paramount Ballroom

Paramount Ballroom

BALLROOM DANCING

9 ⭐ Map p90, D5

This old art deco theatre was the biggest nightclub in Shanghai in the 1930s before transforming into the Red Capital Cinema in the Mao years. An unusual throwback in today's Shanghai, it has low-key tea dances in the afternoon followed by ballroom dancing. (百乐门; 218 Yuyuan Rd; 豫园路218号; tea dances ¥80, ballroom dancing ¥100; ⏱1-4.30pm for tea dances, 4.30-8pm for ballroom dancing; Ⓜ Jing'an Temple)

Shopping

Spin

CERAMICS

10 🔒 Map p90, E3

New-wave, zesty Jingdezhen ceramics are presented in a crisp and trendy space. Reach for fresh, invigorating pieces with cool celadon tones or square teapots and nifty half-glazed tea sets. (旋; 360 Kangding Rd; 康定路360号; ⏱11am-9.30pm; Ⓜ Changping Rd)

Han City Fashion & Accessories Plaza

MARKET, FASHION

11 🔒 Map p90, G4

This unassuming building is a good spot for discount purchases, with

☑ Top Tip

Mobile Communication

Wherever you go in Shanghai, pack a mobile phone. Spoken English is scarce, so don't expect to be understood, even if you speak slowly. From talking to taxi drivers to buying train tickets or in an emergency, have a local contact in Shanghai on speed dial who can do the business for you. A particularly useful number to have is the **Shanghai Call Centre** (☏962 288): it's a free 24-hour English-language hotline that can answer cultural, entertainment or transport enquiries.

hundreds of stalls spread across two floors. Scavenge for shoes, suitcases, sunglasses, shirts, ties and electronics. Bargain hard. (韩城服饰礼品广场; 580 W Nanjing Rd; 南京西路580号; ⊙9am-9pm; Ⓜ W Nanjing Rd)

Amy Lin's Pearls & Jewellery
PEARLS

Oft-visited by dignitaries, Amy Lin's stocks high-quality lustrous salt- and freshwater pearls of all colours, overseen by English-speaking staff who can string them into a choker or a matinée necklace. It's located in the Han City Fashion & Accessories Plaza (see 11 🔒 Map p90, G4). (艾敏林氏珍珠; Room 30, 3rd fl, Han City Fashion & Accessories Plaza, 580 W Nanjing Rd; 南京西路580号3楼30号; ⊙10am-8pm; Ⓜ W Nanjing Rd)

Art Deco
ANTIQUES

You've seen the deco buildings, now peruse the woodwork. This elegant shop, one of several retailers in the M50 complex (see ◉ Map p90, E1), sells stunning furniture from the city's creative heyday, with a few vintage poster girls on the walls to help recapture the 1930s magic. (凹凸家具库; Bldg 7, 50 Moganshan Rd; 莫干山路50号7号楼; ⊙10am-6pm Tue-Sun; Ⓜ Shanghai Railway Station)

Zhang's Textiles
ANTIQUES

12 🔒 Map p90, E4

Some of the brightly coloured antique embroideries on display at Zhang's date to the early Qing dynasty, including divine floral embroidery from the reign of Jia Qing and gorgeous dragon-pattern embroidery from the reign of Dao Guang. (花张; 2nd fl, Shanghai Centre, 1376 W Nanjing Rd; 南京西路1376号; Ⓜ Jing'an Temple or W Nanjing Rd)

Explore

Pudong

Pudong is one of those Chinese place names that most visitors know well before setting foot in Shanghai. In the space of a mere 20 years, the district has gone from boggy farmland to China's economic power-house, a place where Maglev trains glide swiftly into a universe of soaring skyscrapers. Sky-high observation platforms and good museums make it worth the visit.

The Sights in a Day

☀ There's no better way to start a day in Pudong than at the **Shanghai History Museum** (p99), a fun and interactive introduction to the city's past. Once you've absorbed all the history you can handle, it's time to break for lunch, a short walk away at the **Superbrand Mall** (p101).

☀ A hop, skip and three stops down metro line 2 is the Science & Technology Museum. Kids will be interested in the museum itself, but most people shuttle out here for the **AP Xinyang Fashion and Gifts Market** (p119), the city's largest shopping market that also includes pearls and a fabric and tailoring section.

☾ Don't linger too long, as you'll want to get back to a viewing platform before dusk arrives. Head up to the top of one of several skyscrapers in the area – top picks are the **Shanghai World Financial Center** (p99) or the **Jinmao Tower** (p99). Alternatively, stop for a drink in the sky-high bars **Flair** (p101) or **Cloud 9** (p101).

 **Best of Shanghai**

Architecture
Shanghai World Financial Center (p99)

Jinmao Tower (p99)

Oriental Pearl TV Tower (p99)

Museums & Galleries
Shanghai History Museum (p99)

Green Spaces
Riverside Promenade (p99)

Drinking
Flair (p101)

Cloud 9 (p101)

Getting There

Ⓜ **Metro** Line 2 can whisk you through several stations in Pudong, including Lujiazui, Century Ave and the Science & Technology Museum. The former World Expo area is served by line 8; descend at the China Art Museum stop.

🚆 **Bund Sightseeing Tunnel** This thoroughly bizarre **tourist train** (1 way/return ¥50/60) runs between Pudong and the Bund.

N

0   400 m
0   0.2 miles

Daming Rd 大名路

Shanghai Port
International
Ferry Terminal

Xinjian Rd Tunnel 新建路隧道

Ferry Dock

Huángpǔ River

Ferry Dock

Riverside Ave 滨江大道

Middle Yincheng Rd 银城中路

Pearl Garden

Boat Dock

Bund Sightseeing Tunnel

Oriental Pearl TV Tower 4

Lujiazui Ring Rd 陆家嘴环路

Lujiazui Ring Rd 陆家嘴环路

S Pudong Rd 浦东南路

Jing Rd 靖
Changyi Rd 昌邑路

Riverside Promenade 3

Riverside Park

Fenghe Rd 丰和路

Mingzhuta Rd 明珠塔路

Lujiazui 陆家嘴站

W.Lujiazui Rd 陆家嘴西路

Lujiazui Rd

Lujiazui Park 陆家嘴公园

Pudong Ave 浦东大道

Century Ave 世纪大道

E Lujiazui Rd 陆家嘴东路

Qixia Rd 栖霞路

5

6

Huayuanshiqiao Rd 花园石桥路

Jinmao Tower 金茂大厦 2

Dongtai Rd 东泰路

1 Shanghai World Financial Center

Dongchang Rd 东昌路站

Ferry to Pǔdōng

Fucheng Rd 富城路

Lujiazui Ring Rd 陆家嘴环路

Shangcheng Rd 商城路站

E Zhongshan No 2 Rd 中山东二路

Dongchang Rd 东昌路

Ferry Dock

Shangcheng Rd 商城路

Pucheng Rd 浦城路

Fuyou Rd 福佑路

Zhonghua Rd 中华路

Yangshuo Rd 阳朔路

Wutong Rd 梧桐路

Middle Fangbang Rd 方浜中路

Ferry Dock

Ferry Dock

For reviews see

◉ Sights	p99
✕ Eating	p101
🍷 Drinking	p101

Sights

Shanghai World Financial Center
SKYSCRAPER

1 ◉ Map p98, C3

Soon to be deposed by the nearby Shanghai Tower (completion date 2014; height 634m) as the city's tallest building, the neck-craning 492m-high SWFC is an astonishing sight – the observation decks, located at the bottom and top of the trapezoidal hole, are among the world's highest. (上海环球金融中心; www.swfc-observatory.com; 100 Century Ave; 世纪大道100号; observation deck 94th fl ¥120, 97th & 100th fl ¥150; ⊙8am-11pm, last entry 10pm; MLujiazui)

Jinmao Tower
SKYSCRAPER

2 ◉ Map p98, C3

Rising above the clouds, the splendid Jinmao stands beside the shimmering Shanghai World Financial Center like an art-deco pagoda. Shoot to the 88th-floor observation deck to put Shanghai in a splendid nutshell. Time your visit at dusk for both day and night views. Alternatively, sample the same view through the carbonated fizz of a gin and tonic at Cloud 9 (p101). (金茂大厦; 88 Century Ave; 世纪大道88号; observation deck ¥120; ⊙8.30am-9.30pm; MLujiazui)

Shanghai History Museum
MUSEUM

One of Shanghai's top sights, this fun museum charts the city's highs and lows from its days as a cotton-producing town to its grandiose, opium-wreathed heyday and beyond. Life-size models of traditional shops are staffed by realistic waxworks and some exhibits are hands-on or accompanied by creative video presentations. It's located in the Oriental Pearl TV Tower (see **4** ◉ Map p98, B2). (上海城市历史发展陈列馆; Oriental Pearl TV Tower basement; 东方明珠塔; admission ¥35; ⊙8am-9.30pm; MLujiazui)

Riverside Promenade
PROMENADE

3 ◉ Map p98, A3

Hands down the best walk in Pudong, this promenade features full-length views of the Bund in its unfurled, ornate scroll. Choicely positioned cafes and ice-cream stands look out over the water. (滨江大道; ⊙6.30am-11pm; MLujiazui)

Oriental Pearl TV Tower
SKYSCRAPER

4 ◉ Map p98, B2

Love it or hate it, this 468m-tall bauble-adorned tripod has become a symbol of Pudong and the Shanghai renaissance. Join the queue for high-altitude views or head to the basement to visit the highly recommended Shanghai History Museum. (东方明珠广播电视塔; tickets ¥120-298; ⊙8am-10pm; MLujiazui)

Understand

Cultural Hints & Tips

Shanghai, like the rest of China, is not much of a meritocracy: those with *guanxi* (connections) call the shots. Businesspeople invest endless hours in cultivating and massaging (networking) their *guanxi,* normally through business dinners, gift-giving and banqueting.

Another important concept to understand is 'face'. Face can be loosely described as status, ego or self-respect, and is by no means alien to foreigners. Losing face is about making someone look stupid or forcing them to back down in front of others, and you should take care to avoid it. In the West, it's important; in China, it's critical. Circumvent a problem with smiling persistence rather than tackling it straight on, and always give your adversary a way out. Avoid direct criticisms of people. Venting your rage in public and trying to make someone lose face will cause the Chinese to dig in their heels and only worsen your situation. Don't lose sight of your own 'face', however – things should be reciprocal.

Linked to face are displays of respect and politeness. Always offer gifts, cigarettes and food several times, and expect them to be refused several times before finally being accepted.

High density levels and a high tolerance for crowding mean that personal space is generally not a highly valued commodity in Shanghai. No-one is ever going to get a lot of personal space in a country of 1.3 billion people, but the reasons for this are as much cultural as they are physical. Chinese rarely have that sacrosanct 30cm halo of private space around them that foreigners expect. For example, don't expect someone to walk out of your path if you are headed on a collision course.

Whether it be an evening meal out or a day at the park, the Chinese have a preference for things being *'renao'* (literally 'hot and noisy') or lively. This helps explain the penchant for cacophonous banquets and top-volume karaoke sessions. The Shanghai Chinese also put ostentation high on the list. All of this helps explain why Chinese restaurants are often such large, bright, brash and largely unromantic places.

View from Shanghai World Financial Center (p99)

Eating

Superbrand Mall

VARIOUS $$

5 Map p98, B3

This gargantuan, central mall has floors upon floors of restaurants to cater to all tastes and budgets. Head up to the 10th floor for Sichuan-Canto hybrid South Beauty's prime window seats facing the Bund. (正大广场; 168 W Lujiazui Rd; 陆家嘴西路168号; ⊙10am-10pm; MLujiazui)

Drinking

Flair

BAR

6 Map p98, B3

To wow your date (and your bank manager), take the lift to Flair, the highest alfresco terrace in town, for ringside seats onto some of the most sublime neon-scape views of nocturnal Shanghai. (58th fl, Ritz-Carlton Shanghai Pudong, 8 Century Ave; 世纪大道8号58楼; ⊙5.30pm-2am; MLujiazui)

Cloud 9

BAR

Cloud 9 is a fantastic place to watch day fade into night as the lights slowly flicker on across the curving horizon. Access through the Grand Hyatt in the Jinmao Tower (see2 Map p98, C3). (九重天酒廊; 87th fl, Jinmao Tower, 88 Century Ave; 世纪大道88号金茂大厦87楼; ⊙5pm-1am Mon-Fri, 11am-2am Sat & Sun; MLujiazui)

Top Sights
Qibao

Getting There

Qibao is located in western Shanghai.

Ⓜ **Metro** Take line 9 to Qibao station. It's a 20-minute ride from Xujiahui station.

When you tire of Shanghai's incessant quest for modernity, tiny Qibao (七宝) is only a hop, skip and metro ride away. An ancient settlement that prospered during the Ming and Qing dynasties, it is littered with traditional historic architecture, threaded by small, busy alleyways and cut by a picturesque canal. If you can somehow blot out the crowds, Qibao brings you the flavours of old China along with huge doses of entertainment.

Traditional buildings along Qibao's canal

Don't Miss

Cotton Textile Mill

Cotton was Qibao's main industry during the Ming and Qing dynasties. This recreated mill, housed in a former residence, takes you through the entire production process and has displays of old tools, photos and clothing.

Shadow Puppet Museum

This museum provides a brief history of local shadow puppetry, one of China's oldest and most enduring forms of folk art. At its most sophisticated, a travelling troupe would have consisted of five people (the puppeteer, three musicians and a singer). Try to check out the two-hour **performances** (⊙1pm Wed & Sat).

Old Trades House

The Old Trades House is a waxworks museum that introduces the traditional trades practiced in a small Chinese town, from bamboo weaving and fortune-telling to scale making and carpentry.

Zhou's Miniature Carving Gallery

Perhaps the most unusual sight in Qibao is this two-storey gallery, which showcases the miniature carvings of a father and daughter. The highlights are the extraordinarily detailed reproductions of different characters' rooms from the 18th-century classic *Hong Lou Meng* (Dream of Red Mansions).

Other Sights

At No 9 Nan Dajie is a traditional teahouse with **storytelling performances** (admission incl pot of tea ¥2; ⊙12.30-2.30pm), the only one of its kind in Shanghai. Half-hour **boat rides** (per person ¥10; ⊙8.30am-5pm) slowly ferry passengers along the canal. Also worth ferreting out is the **Catholic Church** (天主教堂; 1866), off Qibao Nanjie, south of the canal.

Minhang district;
闵行区

admission ¥45

⊙sights 8.30am-4.30pm

☑ Top Tips

▶ There are nine official sights included in the through ticket, though you can skip the ticket and just pay ¥5 to ¥10 per sight as you go.

✗ Take a Break

At the main bridge, you'll find excellent crab dumplings at **Longpao Xiehuang Tangbao** (龙袍蟹黄汤包; 15 Bei Dajie; 8 dumplings ¥12-28; Ⓜ Qibao).

South of the canal, Nan Dajie is full of snacks and small eateries, such as No 26, which sells sweet *tang yuan* (汤圆) dumplings.

The Best of
Shanghai

Lanterns adorning Yuyuan Gardens (p48)
WULINGYUN/GETTY IMAGES ©

Best Walks
North Bund

🏃 The Walk

The Bund is most famous for the majestic facades that line the Huangpu River, but don't miss the less-known northern end, which is the site of the latest redevelopment project. Known as the Rockbund, the renovations here were funded by the Rockefeller Group and include landmark buildings such as the former British Consulate and the YWCA Building.

Start Broadway Mansions; **M** Tiantong Rd or taxi

Finish Yuanmingyuan Apartments; **M** E Nanjing Rd

Length 800m; 45 minutes

🍴 Take a Break

There aren't any good spots to stop for a break during the tour, but the Bund and its extravagant line-up of bars (p39) and restaurants (p36) is just a few minutes' walk away.

Suzhou Creek, in front of Broadway Mansions

❶ Broadway Mansions

Broadway Mansions was built as an exclusive art deco apartment block in 1934, but, because of its commanding vantage point, it immediately became a favourite with military officers – at first the Japanese, then, after the war, the US.

❷ Astor House Hotel

This landmark edifice was established in 1846 as the Richards Hotel and remained one of Shanghai's most prestigious hotels during the city's golden years. The Shanghai Stock Exchange was headquartered in the hotel's ballroom from 1990 to 1998.

❸ Waibaidu Bridge

Waibaidu Bridge, which crosses Suzhou Creek to connect Hongkou with the Bund, was the first steel bridge in China. An earlier bridge, the Wills' Bridge, built in 1856, levied a toll to cross. Foreigners were apparently allowed to pay on credit, but not the Chinese, and it became renowned as a symbol of foreign oppression.

4 Former British Consulate

The original **British Consulate** was one of the first foreign buildings to go up in Shanghai in 1852, though it was destroyed in a fire and replaced with the current structure in 1873. Also within the grounds are the former **Consul's Residence** (1884) and several century-old magnolia trees.

5 Union Church

There are three surviving heritage buildings on S Suzhou Rd, including the former **Shanghai Rowing Club** (1905) at No 76, the **Church Apartments** (1899) at No 79, and the Romanesque-style **Union Church** (1886) at No 107, which was recently renovated after being damaged in a fire.

6 China Baptist Publication Building

Yuanmingyuan Rd was once home to several godowns – buildings that served as both warehouses and office space. Such buildings were shared by traders and missionaries, such as the 1932 **China Baptist Publication Society**, whose Gothamesque offices at No 187 were designed by the prolific Ladislaus Hudec.

7 Lyceum Building

Other restored buildings along this street include the Italian Renaissance **Lyceum Building** (1927), the multidenominational **Missions Building** (1924; No 169), the lovely **YWCA Building** (1932; No 133) and the red-brick **Yuanmingyuan Apartments** (No 115).

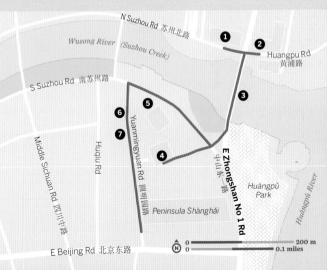

Best Walks
French Concession

🏃 The Walk

The French Concession's leafy backstreets and fabulous architectural diversity provide loads of inspiration for walks. The area is much more residential than the Bund and hence more conducive to leisurely strolls; there are also plenty of tiny boutiques to keep shoppers entertained.

Start All Saints Church; Ⓜ Xintiandi

Finish Cathay Theatre; Ⓜ S Shaanxi Rd

Length 2.5km; 1½ hours

🍴 Take a Break

Sinan Mansions on Middle Fuxing Rd is a convenient place to stop, but if you can hold out, the antique-strewn Lou Shi (p68) on Nanchang Rd has loads more personality.

Sun Yatsen's Former Residence (p64)

❶ All Saints Church

Begin the tour on Middle Fuxing Rd (formerly rue Lafayette), first passing the red-brick Italianate **All Saints Church** (1925) and then the **Park Apartments** (1926) and smaller private villas fronted by large palm trees, which date to the same era.

❷ Former Residence of Liu Haisu

On Middle Fuxing Rd at No 512 is the **Former Residence of Liu Haisu** (1896–1994), a 20th-century artist who revolutionised traditional Chinese art by introducing Western painting styles.

❸ Dubail Apartment Building

The **Dubail Apartment Building** (1931) was the one-time home of US journalist and communist sympathiser Agnes Smedley (1892–1950). Smedley reported extensively on the Chinese civil war in the '30s; her return to the US the following decade was marred by accusations of her being a Soviet spy.

❹ Sinan Mansions

This complex consists of 1920s private villas that were built south of French Park (now Fuxing Park); it was recently renovated as an upscale lifestyle destination. Today it houses numerous cafes and restaurants, as well as ultra-exclusive short-term residences to the south.

❺ Sun Yatsen's Former Residence

A short walk south on Sinan Rd (rte Massenet) is **Zhou Enlai's Former Residence** (No 73),

which served primarily as the Communist Party's Shanghai office. Retrace your footsteps and return along leafy Sinan Rd and its lovely stretch of old villas to reach **Sun Yatsen's Former Residence** (p64), where the father of modern China lived from 1918 to 1924.

❻ Russian Orthodox Church

On Gaolan Rd (rte Cohen) is the **Russian Orthodox Church**, built in 1934 and dedicated to the murdered tsar of Russia.

❼ Nanchang Road

Nanchang Road (rue Vallon) is a popular shopping strip, with a number of boutiques selling jewellery, shoes, antiques and clothing.

❽ Cathay Theatre

Maoming Road (rte Cardinal Mercier) is a shopping hot spot that specialises in tailored *qipao* (cheongsams) and other Chinese-style clothes. Across busy Middle Huaihai Rd is the 1932 **Cathay Theatre**, still in use today as a movie theatre.

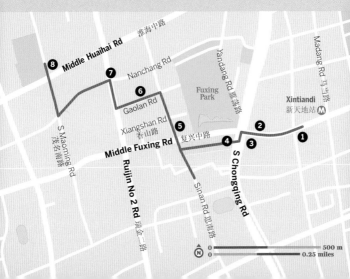

Best
Architecture

Shanghai's sense of self as an erstwhile Paris of the East is inseparable from its architecture. The city is a stuffed treasure chest of architectural styles: Buddhist temple architecture, concession-era villas, homely alleyway houses, grandiose baroque banks, art deco apartment blocks, postmodern towers and dramatic skyscrapers topped with weird sci-fi protuberances. Whatever style floats your boat, Shanghai has it.

Lilong & Shikumen

The Shanghai equivalent of Beijing's charming *hutong* alleyways and courtyard houses are its *lilong* alleys (also called *longtang*) and low-rise *shikumen*, or 'stone-gate houses'.

A distinctive blend of East and West, *shikumen* houses married the traditional Chinese courtyard house – with its interior courtyard features and emphasis on natural light – with the neat brick-work rows of English terrace housing.

Modern Architecture

Since the 1980s a brave new world of architects has been refashioning the Shanghai skyline. The dramatic and modern Pudong skyline, along with parts of Puxi, is testament to the newfound optimism and confidence that now define the city. New edifices such as the Shanghai Tower (under construction) reflect this resurgence that has completely transformed the architectural heritage of Shanghai in under two decades.

WIBOWO RUSLI/GETTY IMAGES ©
SHANGHAI MODERN ARCHITECTURAL DESIGN CO LTD

Best Concession-Era Buildings

Fairmont Peace Hotel An art deco masterpiece and landmark. (p26)

Hongkong & Shanghai Bank Building This neo-classical colossus was once the largest bank in Asia. (p27)

Bank of China Art deco design meets Chinese sensibilities. (p25)

Rockbund Art Museum A winning blend of Chinese and Western ar-chitectural styles. (p36)

Shanghai Art Museum Former Shanghai Race-course Club, with captivating period details. (p36)

Best Shikumen & Lilong Architecture

Bubbling Well Road Apartments Great spot

Fairmont Peace Hotel (p26)

to observe everyday Shanghai life. (p88)

Tianzifang Charming alleyway complex bursting with shops and cafes. (p58)

Xintiandi Shanghai's traditional architectural vernacular re-imagined. (p60)

Best Modern Buildings

Shanghai World Financial Center The tallest building in Shanghai (until 2014). (p99)

Jinmao Tower Eye-catching 88-storey skyscraper in Pudong. (p99)

Shanghai Grand Theatre Shanghai's state-of-the-art concert venue. (p42)

Oriental Pearl TV Tower Pudong's first, and most iconic, tower. (p99)

Best Historic Residences

Sun Yatsen's Former Residence Sun Yatsen lived in this villa from 1918 to 1924. (p64)

Yongfoo Elite No longer a residence, but nonetheless showcases a gorgeous selection of antiques. (p72)

Song Qingling's Former Residence Madame Sun Yatsen's residence after the foundation of the People's Republic of China. (p73)

Mao Zedong's Former Residence Where a young Mao lived in 1924. (p89)

Worth a Trip

Although most of the architecture from the 2010 World Expo has been dismantled, several pavilions are slated to become permanent fixtures in the city skyline. Chief among them is the iconic red China Pavilion, which opened in late 2012 as the **China Art Palace** (中华艺术宫; M China Art Museum, line 8), the city's new modern-art home.

Best
Temples & Churches

To be spellbound by Shanghai's consumer madness is to ignore much of what modern China is about. To get a feel for the Chinese as people, it is vital to have an understanding of their devotional impulses. Religious observance has enjoyed a startling renaissance in Shanghai and the rest of China since the end of Mao Zedong's leadership.

Christianity

China has a long history of importing faiths and beliefs (Buddhism, Judaism, Islam, Christianity, communism), but it is surely Christianity that is making the most converts among modern Chinese. Proselytising may be banned, but this hasn't slowed the spread of the Christian gospel (*hao xiaoxi*) as legions turn to Christianity – partly because associations are made between the religion and the developed-world status of many Christian nations.

Buddhism

Buddhism, too, has enjoyed a considerable upsurge in the past decade, and constitutes the majority of worshippers in Shanghai. The best way to encounter religious observance is to visit the city's temples, such as Jing'an Temple or Jade Buddha Temple.

Best Temples

Jade Buddha Temple Shanghai's most famous Buddhist temple, named after its sublime effigy. (p84)

Chenxiangge Nunnery Gorgeous temple in the Old Town. (p50)

Jing'an Temple Both the oldest and newest temple in Shanghai. (p92)

Confucius Temple Peaceful shrine to the dictum-coining sage in an absorbing neighbourhood. (p53)

TOM HORTON, FURTHER TO FLY PHOTOGRAPHY/GETTY IMAGES ©

Temple of the Town God Revamped Taoist shrine a few steps from the Yuyuan Bazaar. (p49)

Best Churches

Moore Memorial Church Red-brick church on People's Sq designed by Ladislaus Hudec. (p33)

Hongkew Methodist Church Where Song Meiling (May-ling) married Chiang Kaishek in 1927. (p45)

Catholic Church, Qibao Tiny single-steeple church dating from 1867 and attached to a convent. (p103)

Best
Tours

Best Bicycle Tours

BOHDI (📞5266 9013; www.bohdi.com.cn; tours ¥220) Night-time cycling tours on Tuesday (March to November) and trips out of town.

SISU (📞5059 6071; www.sisucycling.com; tours ¥150) Night-time cycling tours on Wednesday and trips out of town.

Best Boat Tours

Huangpu River Cruise – The Bund (黄浦江游览船; 219-239 E Zhongshan No 2 Rd; 中山东二路219-239号; tickets ¥128; ⏰11am-8.30pm) Ninety-minute cruises run from the south end of the Bund (near E Jinling Rd) up to the International Cruise Terminal and back – and then they do it all over again. Try to find a rarer 40- to 60-minute cruise (¥100), which only makes the trip once.

Huangpu River Cruise – Pudong (黄浦江游览船; Pearl Dock; 明珠码头; tickets ¥100; ⏰10am-1.30pm; Ⓜ Lujiazui) Six 40-minute cruises depart from Pudong.

Best Bus & Motorcycle Tours

Big Bus Tours (📞6351 5988; www.bigbustours.com; adult/child US$44/29) Hop-on, hop-off bus services lassoing in the top sights along 22 stops across two routes. Tickets are valid for 48 hours and include a one-hour boat tour of the Huangpu River plus admission to the 88th-floor observation deck of the Jinmao Tower.

City Sightseeing Buses (📞6252 0000; www.springtour.com; tickets ¥30; ⏰9am-8.30pm summer, to 6pm winter) Tickets for these handy hop-on, hop-off, open-top bus tours last 24 hours. The buses offer a convenient way to tour Shanghai's highlights and are a great way to get around the centre of town and Pudong.

PETER ADAMS/GETTY IMAGES ©

Shanghai Sideways (www.shanghaisideways.com; tours from ¥800) Unusual motorcycle-sidecar tours of the city for up to two passengers, setting off from the Peninsula Hotel.

Best
Museums & Galleries

Shanghai devotes considerably more time and energy to fulfilling large infrastructure projects than nurturing a vibrant creative scene, but give the city credit for at least being halfway there: the number of new museums continues to grow with each passing year. Even if you've been to Shanghai before, you'll always have plenty of exhibits to choose from.

KEREN SU/GETTY IMAGES ©

Museums

The landmark cultural institution is the Shanghai Museum (p28), which contains one of the best collections of traditional art in the country. But don't overlook some of the smaller museums or the newer temples to modern art, where you'll get a feel for current social and artistic trends without having to sift through the sometimes mediocre work on display in the galleries.

Galleries

Like many things in Shanghai, Chinese art is a commodity being increasingly vacuumed up by wealthy investors and foreign art hunters. Before you assume there's a genuine artistic revolution out there, it's worth noting the tendency for gallery-hung Chinese art to absorb Western needs and expectations like a multicoloured sponge. Originality is frequently starved and there's still too much pop and not enough hop: the constant ironic artistic references to wealth, communism, propaganda and consumerism can get old fast. But it also means that Shanghai is hardly short of galleries – head to M50 (p86) for the best.

☑ Top Tips

▶ Galleries and public museums (such as the Shanghai Museum) are generally free.

▶ Many museums close their ticket offices 30 to 60 minutes before the venue itself closes.

▶ Students and seniors over 65 are sometimes eligible for discounted admission; take ID.

Best Art Museums

Shanghai Museum
Simply put, Shanghai's best museum. (p28)

Rockbund Art Museum
Top-notch contemporary-art venue. (p36)

Liuli China Museum (p59)

Liuli China Museum
Glass sculpture, from
2000-year-old jewellery to
modern creations. (p59)

**Shanghai Museum
of Contemporary Art
(MOCA Shanghai)** Set in
People's Park. (p36)

**Shanghai Museum of
Arts & Crafts** Shows
crafts such as embroidery
and paper-cutting. (p75)

Best Small Museums

**Shanghai Urban Plan-
ning Exhibition Hall**
Idealised model layout of
the city c 2020. (p36)

**Shanghai History
Museum** Fun, interactive
museum. (p99)

**Shikumen Open House
Museum** See a restored
shikumen house. (p61)

Post Museum Postal
history in imperial China.
(p45)

**CY Tung Maritime
Museum** Model ships
and exhibits on legendary
seafarer Zheng He. (p75)

Best Art Galleries

ShanghART One of
Shanghai's longest-
running galleries. (p87)

Beaugeste Excellent
modern Chinese photog-
raphy. (p59)

island6 Art collective
producing multimedia
installations. (p87)

**Propaganda Poster Art
Centre** Chinese socialist
art from the '50s, '60s
and '70s. (p75)

m97 Photography with
an emphasis on China-
based artists. (p87)

Worth a Trip
Built by the Rus-
sian Ashkenazi
Jewish community
in 1927, the **Ohel
Moishe Syna-
gogue** (摩西会堂;
62 Changyang Rd; 长
阳路62号; admission
¥50; ⊙9am-4.30pm;
Ⓜ Dalian Rd) lies
in the heart of
the 1940s Jewish
ghetto. Today it
houses the Shang-
hai Jewish Refugees
Museum, with
exhibitions on the
lives of the Central
European refugees
who fled to Shang-
hai to escape the
Nazis.

Best
Boutiques

No economic recession here – the Shanghainese have spent the past few years pounding nails into communism's coffin with a vengeance. 'Shop, shop, shop' has become the unofficial mantra, and everyone, from trendy 20-somethings to store-minding grandmothers, is eager to make up for lost time. All the better for visitors: Shanghai shopping has never been so good.

LONELY PLANET/GETTY IMAGES ©

Fashion

The boutiques in the French Concession are where the most interesting finds are going to be, though given the sheer number of tiny shops, it can be hard to separate the wheat from the chaff. Start with shopping strips such as Xinle Rd, which has a good variety of local fashion, and Nanchang Rd, which is good for browsing, with shoes, antiques and clothing. Another good strip is Changle Rd, which has a string of showrooms for up-and-coming designers.

Traditional Chinese Clothing

If you're in the market for a traditional Chinese jacket or *qipao*, you have plenty of tailors to choose from. S Maoming Rd just south of Huaihai Rd is a good place to start comparing designs and patterns; Shanghai 1936 at Tianzifang (p59) is another dependable choice.

Ceramics & Handicrafts

Although Chinese porcelain spent much of the 20th century in an artistic funk, a new generation of designers has started picking up the slack, trying to restore artistic credibility to Jingdezhen ceramics. The results are on display in Shanghai's shops – look for everything from modernist teapots and dinnerware sets to exquisite handmade cups.

☑ **Top Tips**

▶ Most shops are open from 10am to 10pm daily, though smaller boutiques may not open until noon.

Best Boutiques

Tianzifang More shops than you could ever visit in one day. (p59)

NuoMi Gorgeous dresses made from eco-friendly fabrics, including organic cotton and silk. (p79)

XinleLu.com Handpicked bags, shoes and dresses from local designers – plus vintage. (p80)

Heirloom Great place to shop for locally designed handbags with a twist. (p69)

Shopping strip, East Nanjing Road (p32)

PCS (Pop Classic Sneakers) Hip canvas shoes for men, from brands such as Feiyue and Ospop. (p69)

Best Ceramics

Spin New-wave, invigorating ceramics, from kungfu vases to oblong teacups. (p94)

Yu Porcelain from two Jingdezhen designers. (p80)

Blue Shanghai White Small but exquisite collection of hand-painted ceramics. (p43)

Jingdezhen Porcelain Artware High-quality traditional Chinese porcelain. (p89)

Huifeng Tea Shop Quality Yixing teapots and loose-leaf tea. (p69)

Best Local Fashion

Xintiandi Shanghai-style haute couture, from local brands such as la vie and Woo. (p68)

Mayumi Sato Limited-edition Japanese fashion, with sizes that fit Westerners, too. (p81)

Urban Tribe Established eco-conscious label with a lovely tea garden out the back. (p81)

Annabel Lee Peruse the collection of shawls, scarves, bags and table runners, most of which feature hand-stitched embroidery. (p42)

Madame Mao's Dowry Retro motifs and designer clothing. (p81)

Best Jewellery & Handicrafts

Amy Lin's Pearls & Jewellery High-quality salt- and freshwater pearls at unbeatable prices. (p95)

Brocade Country Charming collection of handicrafts from China's southwest. (p81)

Nine Exquisite line of handmade Tibetan-themed jewellery. (p69)

Suzhou Cobblers Hand-embroidered silk slippers. (p43)

Yunhong Chopsticks Shop Smart little shop selling designer chopsticks. (p33)

Best
Markets & Antiques

For variety and the best deals, roll up your sleeves at Shanghai's markets. Whether you're looking for tailor-made clothes, bargain T-shirts or caged crickets, nothing can beat the sensory overload of a local market. Haggling is the norm, so make sure you test the waters before making a purchase, or you could wind up paying over-the-top prices.

Tailor-Made Clothes

If you're worried about finding the right size, the Old Town fabric markets may be the solution. All manner of textiles can be found here, from synthetic to silk and cashmere – compare fabric and prices at different stands to ensure no one is blatantly ripping you off. Suits, pants, shirts, dresses and scarves can be made at such places in as little as 24 hours (expect to pay extra), though a one-week turnaround is more realistic.

Counterfeits

'In Shanghai, everything can be faked except for your mother', or so the saying goes. Counterfeit goods are ubiquitous; even if you've set out to buy a genuine item, there's no guarantee that that's what you're going to get. Antiques in particular are almost always reproductions: the best word of advice is to buy something because you like it, not because you think it has historic value.

Haggling

In the markets, haggling over prices is all part of the shopping experience. In particularly touristy places, you can usually get the price to drop by at least 50%, and sometimes even 75%.

GREG ELMS/GETTY IMAGES ©

☑ Top Tips

▶ Technically, nothing over 200 years old can be taken out of China, but you'll be very lucky if you come across any antiques that old in Shanghai. If you are buying a reproduction, make sure the dealer provides paperwork stating that it is not an antique.

Best Antiques

Old Street Excellent range of souvenirs, such as reproduced calendar posters. (p51)

Dongtai Road Antique Market Over 100 stalls wedged between the Old Town and the French Concession. (p55)

Shiliupu Fabric Market (p51)

Art Deco Stylish period furnishings that match the Fairmont Peace Hotel's streamlined aplomb. (p95)

Lou Shi Cafe and antique shop. (p68)

Fuyou Antique Market This place is at its best during the weekend 'ghost market'. (p51)

Best Clothing Markets

Shiliupu Fabric Market Cashmere coats, silk shirts and dresses tailor-made for a song. (p51)

Han City Fashion & Accessories Plaza Scavenge for bargain bags, T-shirts, pearls and more. (p94)

Qipu Market The go-to market for the lowest prices in town. (p45)

Best Traditional Markets

Flower, Bird, Fish & Insect Market Prize-fighting crickets, turtles, songbirds and bonsai. (p53)

Tanggu Road Food Market Live crabs and fish, pickled vegetables, mangoes, lychees and thousand-year-old eggs. (p45)

Worth a Trip

One-stop shopping in all its bargain-basement glory is found in the **AP Xinyang Fashion and Gifts Market** (亚太新阳服饰礼品市场; ◷10am-8pm; ⓂScience & Technology Museum), located in the Science & Technology Museum metro station. There's an entire fabric market here (for tailored clothing), rows upon rows of pearls, plus all the usual suspects: shoes, sports equipment, T-shirts, electronics... Bargain hard.

Best
Entertainment

BRUNO MORANDI/GETTY IMAGES ©

Shanghai is no longer the city of sin that went out dancing as the revolution shot its way into town, but the entertainment options have blossomed once more over the past decade. Plug in to the local cultural scene for a stimulating shot of jazz concerts, acrobatics or traditional Chinese music.

Acrobatics

Shanghai troupes are among the best in the world and spending a night watching them spinning plates on poles and contorting themselves into unfeasible anatomical positions never fails to entertain. See www.shanghaiacrobaticshow.com for an overview of performances around town.

Music

Shanghai had a brief heyday in the jazz spotlight, back in the 1920s and '30s when big-band swing was the entertainment of choice. It remains a popular genre and even if you won't catch many household names, there are some surprisingly good musicians here.

Best Local Entertainment

Shanghai Centre Theatre Acrobatics performances. (p93)

Bandu Cabin Traditional Chinese music performances on Saturday. (p93)

PartyWorld For the ultimate China experience, you just can't beat karaoke. (p67)

Yifu Theatre Catch a Beijing opera highlights show here. (p42)

Shanghai Grand Theatre From musicals and international orchestras to dance and theatre. (p42)

Best Rock & Jazz

Fairmont Peace Hotel Jazz Bar Featuring

☑ **Top Tips**

▶ Tickets for all of the city's performing-arts events can be purchased at the venues where the performances take place; also check www.culture.sh.cn or www.smartshanghai.com/smartticket.

Shanghai's most famous jazz band. (p42)

MAO Livehouse The city's largest venue for rock and indie concerts. (p68)

Cotton Club The longest-running jazz and blues bar in Shanghai. (p79)

JZ Club Jazz bar showcasing a wide range of styles, from big band to groove. (p79)

Best
Massage & Spas

In Shanghai, a body or foot massage will come at a fraction of the price that you'd pay at home. Options range from neighbourhood foot-massage parlours – where everyone kicks back on an armchair and watches TV – to midrange and luxury hotel spas, which offer private rooms, a change of clothes and a wonderfully soothing atmosphere.

EIGHTFISH/GETTY IMAGES ©

Best Massage Parlours

Dragonfly (悠庭保健会所; ☎5405 0008; www.dragonfly.net.cn; 20 Donghu Rd; 东湖路20号; ⏰10am-2am; Ⓜ S Shaanxi Rd) One of the longest-running massage services in Shanghai, the peaceful Dragonfly offers Chinese body massages, foot massages and Japanese-style shiatsu in addition to more specialised services, such as aroma oil massages and beauty treatments. Reserve.

Green Massage (青专业按摩; ☎5386 0222; www.greenmassage.com.cn; 58 Taicang Rd; 太仓路58号; ⏰10.30am-2am; Ⓜ S Huangpi Rd) Calming fragrances envelop guests at this plush midrange spa, which offers foot, *tuina* and shiatsu massages. In addition to traditional practices such as cupping and moxibustion, it also provides waxing and other beauty treatments. Reserve.

Green Massage (☎6289 7776; 2nd fl, Shanghai Centre, 1376 W Nanjing Rd; 南京西路1376号; ⏰10.30am-2am; Ⓜ Jing'an Temple) Jing'an branch. Reserve.

Double Rainbow Massage House (双彩虹保健按摩厅; 45 Yongjia Rd; 永嘉路45号; ⏰noon-midnight; Ⓜ S Shaanxi Rd) Perhaps Shanghai's best neighbourhood massage parlour, the visually impaired masseuses here will have you groaning in agony in no time as they seek out those oft-neglected pressure points. The rates are a steal.

Best
Food

GREG ELMS/GETTY IMAGES ©

Shanghai is the white-hot crucible of China's economic makeover, and the fizzing sense of excitement also fires up its kitchens. The city is as much a magnet for regional Chinese chefs as it is for superstar toques from around the globe, and has staked a formidable claim as the Middle Kingdom's trendiest dining destination.

Shanghainese

You can't come to Shanghai without sampling its own, celebrated local cuisine, which is generally sweeter than other Chinese cuisines. Standout dishes to try include braised pork belly (红烧肉), drunken chicken (醉鸡), smoked fish (熏鱼) and the local dumpling varieties: *xiaolongbao* (小笼包; steamed or soup dumplings) and *shengjian* (生煎; fried dumplings).

Regional Chinese

China's a big, big place, but luckily its flavours converge in Shanghai. You don't have to trek to far-flung Kashgar for Uighur noodles or Hunan for Mao's stewed pork. Spicy Sichuanese restaurants have come to town, so there's no need to hoof it to Chengdu, while Yunnanese chefs have shuttled in from Kunming. Don't be afraid to experiment – there's sure to be plenty you can't find at home, so do as the Shanghainese do and dig in with those chopsticks!

☑ Top Tips

▶ Tipping is not done in the majority of restaurants. High-end international restaurants are another matter: while tipping is not obligatory, it is encouraged.

▶ Most of the listings in this guide have English and/or picture menus.

▶ Reservations a few days in advance are necessary for more popular restaurants.

Best Shanghainese

Jesse (Xinjishi) Shanghainese home cooking in all its sweet and oily glory. (p65, p77)

Fu 1039 Old-fashioned charm and succulent Shanghainese. (p76)

T8 (p67)

Baoluo Jiulou Unpretentious favourite that's been going strong for decades. (p77)

Ye Shanghai Elegant presentation and 1930s decor. (p67)

Bai's Restaurant Family-run restaurant. (p77)

Best Regional Chinese

Di Shui Dong Countryside cookin' and Hunanese chilli peppers. (p64)

Yin MSG-free regional cuisine in a romantic setting. (p75)

Lost Heaven Trendy Yunnanese specialities. (p36)

Cha's Travel back in time to a 1950s Hong Kong diner. (p65)

Best Dumplings

Din Tai Fung Sophisticated street food from Taiwan. (p53, p64)

Yang's Fry Dumplings Simple, greasy and oh so good. (p38)

Nanxiang Steamed Bun Restaurant The oldest *xiaolongbao* chain in Shanghai. (p38)

Yunnan Road Food Street Shaanxi dumplings, cold noodles, five-fragrance dim sum and more. (p37)

Crystal Jade Great for Singapore- and Shanghai-style dim sum. (p65)

Best Vegetarian

Vegetarian Lifestyle Hip, delicious and organic, too. (p92)

Jade Buddha Temple Eat with the monks and nuns. (p85)

Qimin Organic Hotpot Healthy, refined hotpots for gourmands. (p93)

Songyuelou Shanghai's oldest vegie restaurant. (p55)

Best Gastronomic

Mr & Mrs Bund Re-imagined French bistro fare for night owls. (p38)

el Willy Creative tapas and Catalan cool. (p38)

M on the Bund The grande dame of Shanghai dining. (p39)

T8 Seductive *shikumen* setting and Sichuan high pie. (p67)

Best
Drinking

LONELY PLANET/GETTY IMAGES ©

Shanghai loves its lychee martinis and cappuccinos to go, and with such exclusive tastes, it's no surprise that even former basketball star Yao Ming has decided to get in on the action with his own Cabernet Sauvignon brand. But don't be intimidated by the glitzy exterior: underneath is a happening nightlife scene that keeps everyone – VIP or not – well entertained.

Bars

Shanghai has stayed true to its roots: it's all about looking flash, sipping craft cocktails or imported wine, and tapping into the insatiable appetite for new trends. New bars pop up and disappear with impressive rapidity, but the upside to the competition is that weekly specials and happy hours (generally from 5pm to 8pm) help keep the city affordable.

Cafes

Cafe culture is the latest rage to sweep Shanghai and, though you'd be hard pressed to find a decent teahouse within a 20km radius, lattes and sandwiches served at hip wireless hangouts are all over the place. Another common sight are the street stalls selling bubble tea, a Taiwanese milk tea with tapioca balls, and all sorts of related spin-offs, such as hot ginger drinks or freshly pureed papaya smoothies.

Clubbing

Shanghai's clubs are mostly big, glossy places devoted to playing mainstream house, techno and hip-hop. A number of big-name DJs have helped boost interest among locals, although the crowds are still mainly made up of Westerners, Hong Kong and Taiwanese expats, and young, rich Shanghainese. Check local listings for the latest hot spots.

☑ Top Tips

▶ Many bars offer a full dining menu and open for lunch at 11am. Bars that only serve drinks are more erratic; they might open anywhere between 4.30pm and 8pm. Last call is between 2am and 5am.

▶ Clubs generally don't get going until 10pm and stay open until 5am on weekends.

Best Design

Long Bar Colonial-era decor and old-fashioned cocktails. (p39)

Old Shanghai Teahouse For a taste of 1930s Shanghai. (p51)

Glamour Bar (p39)

Bar Rouge Chic Bund lounge, with electro beats and ruby-red lighting. (p41)

Apartment Hip bar with drinks, dining and dancing. (p78)

Barbarossa Escape to this oasis in People's Park. (p39)

Best Views

Flair The highest alfresco seats in the city. (p101)

Cloud 9 Although indoors, Cloud 9 still gives Flair a run for its money. (p101)

New Heights The definitive angle on Pudong's electric skyline. (p39)

Captain's Bar For low-budget seats and a glam-free atmosphere. (p39)

M1nt This exclusive penthouse lounge is the ultimate see-and-be-seen destination. (p42)

Best Cocktails

Glamour Bar Marvellous martinis and first-rate events. (p39)

el Cóctel Retro cocktail lounge with perfectionist barkeeps. (p78)

Alchemist Drinks for magicians and mad scientists. (p67)

Fennel Sunken bar, live music and grown-up vibe. (p79)

Best Pubs

Abbey Road Cheap drinks, decent pub grub and classic rock. (p78)

Cotton's The French Concession villa everyone wants to call home. (p78)

Kaiba Shanghai's imported-beer specialist. (p67)

Shanghai Brewery Gargantuan microbrewery with dining, and live sports on TV. (p79)

Best Cafes

Café 85°C Sea-salt coffee and frothy green tea. (p89)

Lou Shi Soothing antique-strewn atmosphere. (p68)

Wagas Shanghai's own wi-fi equipped cafe chain. (p93)

Best Clubs

Shelter Underground beats in an old bomb shelter. (p78)

No 88 Over-the-top party atmosphere. (p78)

Best
Gay & Lesbian
Shanghai

NATIONAL GEOGRAPHIC/GETTY IMAGES ©

Shanghai's gay scene is low profile: the Chinese are a naturally undemonstrative people, their culture is conservative and the Communists put gay pride way down on their wish list. With considerable stigma attached to homosexuality, openly coming out is far more difficult in Chinese society than it is elsewhere in the world. Yet, as a rapidly liberalising city, Shanghai is a natural destination for China's gays and lesbians. *City Weekend* runs a bimonthly gay and lesbian column.

Best Gay Venues

Shanghai Studio (www.shanghai-studio.com; No 4, Lane 1950, Middle Huaihai Rd; 淮海中路1950弄4号; ⏰9pm-2am; Ⓜ Jiaotong University) This hip addition to the Shanghai gay scene has transformed the cool depths of a former bomb shelter into a laid-back bar, art gallery and men's underwear shop (MANifesto; open 2pm to 2am).

Eddy's Bar (☏6282 0521; 1877 Middle Huaihai Rd; 淮海中路1877号; ⏰8pm-2am; Ⓜ Jiaotong University) Shanghai's longest-running gay bar is a friendly place with a flash square bar to sit around, as well as a few corners to hide away in.

390 Bar (www.390shanghai.com; 390 Panyu Rd; 番禺路390号; ⏰6pm-late; 📶; Ⓜ Jiaotong University) One of the only LGBT clubs in Shanghai, with live music, DJs and great cocktails.

Aromassage (茗之荟; ☏6267 0783; 38 Changhua Rd; 昌化路38号; ⏰11am-1am; Ⓜ W Nanjing Rd) Inexpensive but excellent foot and body massages.

Best
Taichi & Martial Arts

Dreaming of upending hardened karate fourth-*dan* black belts with a mere shrug? Itching to master the devastating eight palm changes of Bagua Zhang? Now is your chance. For many young Chinese, learning martial arts is about as sexy as watching paint dry, but the mind-bending antics of Bruce Lee and Jackie Chan have fired up generations of eager Westerners.

GREG ELMS/GETTY IMAGES ©

Good places to look for teachers and students are Shanghai's parks, first thing in the morning. If you ask to join a group of practitioners, you'll usually be welcomed.

Best Martial Arts Schools

Longwu Kungfu Center (龙武功夫馆; ☎ 6287 1528; www.longwukungfu.com; 1 S Maoming Rd; 茂名南路1号; Ⓜ S Shaanxi Rd) Coaches from Shanghai's martial arts teams give classes in Chinese, Japanese and Korean martial arts. The largest centre in the city, it also offers children's classes on weekend mornings and lessons in English.

Wuyi Chinese Kungfu Centre (武懿国术馆; ☎ 137 0168 5893; Room 311, 3rd fl, International Artists' Factory, No 3, Lane 210, Taikang Rd; 法租界泰康路210弄3号3楼311; Ⓜ Dapuqiao) English-language taichi classes on Thursday and Sunday and *wushu* classes on Wednesday and Sunday for adults and kids.

Mingwu International Kungfu (明武国际功夫馆; ☎ 6465 9806; www.mingwukungfu.com; 3rd fl, Hongchun Bldg, 3213 Hongmei Rd; 虹梅路3213号红春大厦3楼) This versatile gym offers bilingual classes in a wide range of martial arts, from taichi and qigong to *wushu* and karate, for both children and adults.

Best
For Kids

PAUL SOUDERS/GETTY IMAGES ©

Shanghai isn't exactly at the top of most kids' holiday wish lists, but the new Disney theme park in Pudong (estimated completion date 2015) will no doubt improve its standing. In the meantime, if you're passing through the city with children, the following sights will keep the family entertained.

In addition to the sights listed below, check out these other possibilities online: **Happy Valley** (sh.happyvalley.cn), **Dino Beach** (www.64783333.com), **Science & Technology Museum** (www.sstm.org.cn) and the **Shanghai Ocean Aquarium** (www.sh-aquarium. com). Bus tours are a good option for getting around the city.

☑ **Top Tips**

▶ In general, 1.4m is the cut-off height for children's tickets. Children under 0.8m normally get in for free.

▶ The popularity of kids' attractions everywhere peaks on holidays and weekends, but in China, 'crowded' takes on a new meaning. Try to schedule your visits for weekdays if possible.

Best Children's Activities

Shanghai World Financial Center Ascend supersonic elevators to the sky-high observation decks. (p99)

Jinmao Tower A less-expensive viewing platform than the Financial Center. (p99)

Shanghai History Museum Wax figures and interactive exhibits make this a family-friendly museum. (p99)

Shanghai Centre Theatre An evening of plate-spinning and contortionism never fails to entertain. (p93)

Shanghai Zoo (上海动物园; www.shanghaizoo.cn; 2381 Hongqiao Rd; 虹桥路 2381号; adult/child ¥40/20; ⊙6.30am-6pm Apr-Sep, to 5pm Oct-Mar; Ⓜ Shanghai Zoo) As Chinese zoos go, this is just about the best there is. In addition to the animals, there are acres of green space to run around in.

Best
For Free

Shanghai is the most expensive city in China, bar Hong Kong. And as inflation and the value of the yuan continue to climb, it's only going to become more so. Whether you're on a budget or just want to save your pennies, make sure you check out these recommendations.

Cheap Eats

Shanghai's restaurants are in a whole other ballpark when compared to the rest of China – meal prices here even exceed Beijing's, and to top it off, the portions are smaller! Thankfully, you can still eat cheaply if you know where to look. Malls are always a good place to begin; check the basement or top floors for food courts. Street food is another good bet – dumpling stalls and noodle shops generally offer the cheapest meals in the city.

More and more restaurants catering to office workers offer good-value weekday lunch specials: to take advantage, ask for a *taocan* (套餐).

Film Screenings

A handful of bars and cafes around town screen weekly films for free. Check local mags for the monthly schedule.

Best Museums

Shanghai Museum
Simply put, Shanghai's best museum. (p28)

Bund History Museum
Introduces Bund history through old photographs and maps. (p25)

Best Communist Heritage

Site of the 1st National Congress of the CCP Certainly not the most enthralling attraction, but a must for political-history buffs. Passport required. (p61)

Mao Zedong's Former Residence Traditional *shikumen* architecture and Mao memorabilia. Passport required. (p89)

M50 The largest complex of modern-art galleries in Shanghai. (p86)

Post Museum Surprisingly interesting, with great views. (p45)

CY Tung Maritime Museum Learn more about 15th-century explorer Zheng He here. (p75)

Best
Green Spaces

Although at first glance Shanghai seems to be as concrete as they come, with a little exploration you can find some pleasant acres of greenery and some nicely landscaped areas. Like the historic architecture, Shanghai's main parks are generally European in layout, though the flora is primarily native, with lots of magnolia trees, fatsia and bamboo.

The most central green space is People's Park, located on the northern half of People's Sq. Built on the site of the colonial racetrack, the park is a leafy refuge in the heart of the city, and is home to two museums and a pond-side cafe-bar. If you're in Shanghai in June, look out for the pink lotus flowers in the pond.

If you want to picnic on the grass or volley a football around, however, you're out of luck. Shanghai's modern parks are largely synthetically designed, with concrete trimming and recurrent keep-off-the-grass notices (hence the woeful state of Chinese football). Larger parks include the Shanghai Zoo and Zhongshan Park in the west of town.

PETER STUCKINGS/GETTY IMAGES ©

Best Parks

Fuxing Park Once known as French Park, Fuxing Park is an excellent spot to look for early-morning taichi classes. (p64)

Huangpu Park China's first modern park, laid out in 1866. It's located on the Bund. (p25)

Riverside Promenade This Pudong walkway looks back towards the Bund and is a pleasant stroll, lined with cafes and ice-cream stands. (p99)

Survival Guide

Survival Guide

Before You Go

When to Go

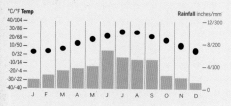

➡ **Winter (Dec–Feb)**
Cold and clammy. Chinese New Year comes in with a bang in January or February.

➡ **Spring (Mar–May)**
Temperatures start to rise. Late April and May are pleasant, but avoid major holidays.

➡ **Summer (Jun–Aug)**
Rainfall in Shanghai hits its peak in June, just as the sweltering summer heat arrives.

➡ **Autumn (Sep–Nov)**
This is one of the best times to visit, as temperatures drop from summer highs.

Book Your Stay

☑ **Top Tip** Always take your hotel's business card with you when you go out for the day. You will need to show the Chinese address to your driver if you return via taxi.

➡ Shanghai's sleeping options are excellent at either end of the spectrum, though quality in the midrange market remains in short supply – do your homework and secure a room well ahead of time.

➡ Don't pass over top-end hotels; competition and heavy discounts mean rates are often reasonable.

➡ Four- and five-star hotels add a 10% or 15% service charge, which is sometimes negotiable.

➡ Save money by staying at a Chinese chain (eg Motel 168) or in a private double in a hostel.

➡ Even if you're not a backpacker, don't be put off the idea of staying in a hostel. Private doubles are cheaper (and often better) than rooms in locally run midrange hotels, and the level of service is much higher, as staff are sure to speak English.

➡ Hotels listed here have air-conditioning, broadband internet access and/or wi-fi.

Useful Websites

CTrip (http://english.ctrip.com) Reliable site for hotel and domestic-flight bookings.

Elong (www.elong.net) Reliable site for hotel and domestic-flight bookings.

Lonely Planet (www.lonelyplanet.com/hotels) Author-penned reviews and online booking.

Best Budget

Mingtown Nanjing Road Youth Hostel (南京路青年旅舍; www.yhachina.com) The newest Bund-side hostel.

Le Tour Traveler's Rest (乐途静安国际青年旅舍; www.letourshanghai.com) Bundles of space and old-Shanghai textures.

Mingtown E-Tour Youth Hostel (新易途国际青年旅舍; www.yhachina.com) Choice location just behind People's Sq and a tranquil courtyard.

Mingtown Hiker Youth Hostel (旅行者青年旅馆; www.yhachina.com) Well-located dorms a short hop from the Bund.

Motel 168 (莫泰连锁旅馆; www.motel168.com) Modern doubles, and the price is right.

Best Midrange

Astor House Hotel (浦江饭店; www.astorhousehotel.com) Great location and old-world charm.

Quintet (www.quintet -shanghai.com) Chic B&B with modern design.

Marvel Hotel (商悦青年会大酒店; www.marvelhotels.com.cn) Located in the former YMCA building off People's Sq.

Magnolia Bed & Breakfast (www.magnoliabnbshanghai.com) Cosy B&B in a 1927 French Concession home.

Kevin's Old House (老时光酒店; www.kevinsoldhouse.com) Lovely French Concession boutique hotel with stylish suites.

Best Top End

Fairmont Peace Hotel (费尔蒙和平饭店; www.fairmont.com) The city's most famous hotel, renovated in all its art deco magic.

Langham Xintiandi (新天地朗廷酒店; www.langhamhotels.com) Top-of-the-line French Concession luxury.

Urbn (www.urbnhotels.com) China's first carbon-neutral hotel.

Ritz-Carlton Shanghai Pudong (www.ritzcarlton.com) The best of Pudong's skyscraping suites.

Peninsula (上海半岛酒店; www.peninsula.com) Historic elegance meets modern comfort on the Bund.

Arriving in Shanghai

☑ **Top Tip** For the best way to get to your accommodation, see p17.

Pudong International Airport

Pudong International Airport (PVG; 浦东国际机场; ✈ flight info 96990; www.shairport.com) is 30km southeast of Shanghai, and handles all international flights. There are four ways to get from the airport to the city: Maglev train, taxi, metro and bus.

➡ The quickest way into the city is on the bullet-fast **Maglev** (with same-day air ticket ¥40; ⏱ 6.45am-9.40pm), which takes just eight minutes to Pudong and is a considerable time-saver. Once you arrive at the terminus (Longyang Rd), you will need to transfer to metro line 2 or take a taxi the rest of the way. If you go by taxi, be sure to look for the meter when you get in the car; if the counter is hidden by a receipt, switch cabs. You should pay ¥40 to ¥60 to downtown Shanghai (People's Sq).

➡ A taxi ride from the airport to central Shanghai will cost around ¥160 and take about an hour. Take a cab from the official taxi rank and make sure the meter is visible when you get in.

➡ Metro line 2 runs to central Shanghai and is the cheapest way to get to town (¥7 to People's Sq, 75 minutes). About halfway through your trip, you will need to switch trains (but not metro lines) at Guanglan Rd in Pudong. Service to the airport runs from 6.30am to 9pm. If you have an evening departure, you must be *at* Guanglan Rd by 9pm or you will miss

the last metro to the airport.

➡ Buses run from the airport, taking between 60 and 90 minutes to reach their destinations in central Shanghai. Buses leave the airport from 6.30am to 11pm; they go to the airport from 5.30am to 9.30pm (bus 1 runs till 11pm). The most useful buses are airport bus 1 (¥30), which links Pudong International Airport with Hongqiao Airport, and airport bus 2 (¥22), which links Pudong International Airport with the Airport City Terminal, east of Jing'an Temple.

Hongqiao Airport

Hongqiao Airport (SHA; 虹桥机场; ☑ flight info 96990; www.shairport. com) serves domestic destinations and is 18km west of the Bund, a 30- to 60-minute trip.

➡ Most flights now arrive at Terminal 2, which is connected to downtown via metro lines 2 and 10 (30 minutes to People's Sq).

➡ If you arrive at Terminal 1, you can also catch the airport shuttle bus (¥4, 7.50am to 11pm) to the

Airport City Terminal, east of Jing'an Temple.

➡ Taxis cost ¥70 to ¥100 to central Shanghai.

Hongqiao Railway Station

Hongqiao Railway Station (上海虹桥站; Ⓜ Hongqiao Railway Station) is adjacent to Hongqiao Airport. It's the terminus for the Shanghai–Beijing express; new express trains to Nanjing and Suzhou also leave from here. It is served by metro lines 2 and 10.

Shanghai Railway Station

Trains depart to destinations all over China from the **Shanghai Railway Station** (上海火车站; Ⓜ Shanghai Railway Station). Trains from Hong Kong also arrive here. It is served by metro lines 1, 3 and 4.

Shanghai South Railway Station

Trains from certain southern destinations, such as Hangzhou, arrive at the **Shanghai South Railway Station** (上海南站; Ⓜ Shanghai South Railway Station). It is served by metro lines 1 and 3.

Getting Around

Metro

☑ **Best for**... General travel throughout Shanghai. This book indicates the nearest metro station after the Ⓜ in each listing.

➡ The city's metro, indicated by a large red M, is the best way to get around Shanghai. It is fast, cheap and clean, although don't count on getting a seat. There should be 14 lines in operation by the time this book is in print – up from three lines in 2003!

➡ The most useful lines for travellers are 1, 2 and 10.

➡ Tickets range from ¥3 to ¥10 depending on the distance; they are sold from the bilingual automated machines. Keep your ticket until you exit.

➡ Most trains run from about 5.30am to 10.30pm.

Taxi

☑ **Best for**... Reaching destinations not located near metro stops, and for travelling after 10.30pm.

Tickets & Passes

A one-/three-day metro pass is sold at the airports and from some information desks for ¥18/45. Otherwise, if you are going to be doing a lot of travelling in Shanghai, it's worth investing in a transport card (交通卡). Sold at metro stations and some convenience stores, these handy cards can be filled up with credit and used on the metro and most buses and in taxis. You'll need to pay a deposit of ¥20, which can be refunded before you leave at the E Nanjing Rd metro station.

➡ Shanghai's taxis are reasonably cheap, hassle-free and easy to flag down outside rush hour, although finding a cab during rainstorms is impossible.

➡ Flag fall is ¥14 (for the first 3km) and ¥18 at night (11pm to 5am). For the most part, Shanghai's cabbies are honest, but make sure you can see the meter when you get in the car and that it is turned on.

➡ To overcome the language barrier, always take the Chinese address of your destination (included in this guide). If need be, call a local contact or the **Shanghai Call Centre** (📞 962 288; ⏱24hr), an English-language hotline, to help you communicate.

➡ If you feel you've been cheated, make sure you get a receipt and the cab driver's ID number, then call the company to file a complaint. The main taxi companies are **Dazhong** (📞 96822), **Bashi** (📞 96840) and **Qiang-sheng** (📞 6258 0000).

Essential Information

Business Hours

☑ **Top Tip** Final entry to many museums is generally half an hour to an hour before the official closing time.

➡ Banks are normally open Monday to Friday

from 9am to noon and about 2pm to 4.30pm. Most banks have 24-hour ATMs. Some branches also open on Saturday morning.

➡ Restaurants are open from 11am to 10pm or later. Fancier places close for an afternoon break at about 2.30pm before opening again from 5pm to 11pm or later.

➡ Department stores are generally open from 10am to 10pm; smaller boutiques may not open until noon but generally stay open until 9pm or 10pm.

➡ Some bars open for lunch, others open at about 5pm. Last call is generally 2am, but there are a handful of places that stay open until dawn.

Discount Cards

➡ Students and seniors over the age of 65 often qualify for reduced admission. You will need to provide ID as proof.

Electricity

See p16 for detailed information.

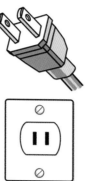

220V/50Hz

220V/50Hz

Emergency

Ambulance (☎120)

Fire (☎119)

Police (☎110)

Money

☑ **Top Tip** Remember to always retrieve your card after using an ATM. You can access your cash without taking your card back, hence it's easy to forget that it's in the machine.

➡ The Chinese currency is known as Renminbi (RMB). The basic unit of RMB is the yuan (¥). For updated currency exchange rates, check www.xe.com.

➡ It's easiest to use cash in Shanghai; ATMs that take foreign cards are widespread. Look for the Bank of China (中国银行), Industrial and Commercial Bank of China (ICBC; 工商银行) and HSBC (汇丰银行), many of which have 24-hour ATMs. Many top-end hotels, shopping malls and department stores also have ATMs.

➡ Credit cards are accepted more in Shanghai than elsewhere in China. Most tourist hotels will accept major credit cards, as will banks, high-end restaurants and international boutiques.

Public Holidays

The following are the main public holidays in China:

New Year's Day 1 January

Chinese New Year 31 January 2014, 19 February 2015; a week-long break, also known as Spring Festival

Tomb Sweeping Day First weekend in April; three-day weekend

International Labour Day 1 May; three-day weekend

Dragon Boat Festival 12 June 2013, 2 June 2014

Mid-Autumn Festival 19 September 2013, 8 September 2014

National Day 1 October; officially three days but often morphs into a week-long holiday

Safe Travel

➜ Shanghai feels very safe, and crimes against foreigners are rare. Crossing the road is probably the greatest danger: develop avian vision and a sixth sense to guard against the traffic.

➜ If any of your possessions are stolen, you need to report the crime at the district Public Security Bureau (PSB; 公安局) office and obtain a police report.

Telephone

☑ **Top Tip** Buy a cheap, unlocked GSM phone to use for international travel. That way you can simply buy a SIM card once you arrive at your destination and you'll be good to go.

Mobile Phones

➜ Inexpensive pay-as-you-go SIM cards are available for unlocked GSM phones. If your phone is not compatible (eg Verizon customers in the US), buying or renting a local phone may be a better option than international roaming plans.

➜ The main service providers are China Mobile (中国移动) and China Unicom (中国联通), both of which have sales counters at Pudong International Airport (arrivals hall) and around Shanghai.

➜ You can buy SIM cards at some convenience stores and magazine kiosks; cheap phones can be found at electronics markets.

➜ If you prefer to rent a mobile phone (you'll still need to buy a SIM card), you can get one at Pudong International Airport or online (www.pandaphone.com). It will probably cost about US$50 for a week, including all fees and the SIM card.

Money-Saving Tips

➜ Many public museums are free – see p129.

➜ Chinese chain hotels such as Motel 168 and Jinjiang Inn are generally of reasonable quality and considerably cheaper than most other Shanghai hotel rooms.

➜ A handful of bars and cafes around town screen weekly films for free. Check local mags for the monthly schedule.

➜ Always check out malls for convenient and relatively inexpensive dining options.

Phonecards

➡ IC (integrated circuit) cards (IC卡; *IC ka*) can be used for local and (expensive) international calls in public street phones, Telecom offices and most hotels.

➡ Internet phonecards (IP cards; IP卡; *IP ka*), purchased at newspaper kiosks, are much cheaper for international calls; use any home phone, some hotel phones and some public phones (but not card phones) to dial a special telephone number and follow the instructions. Check you have the right card for use in Shanghai.

Country & City Codes

Note the following country and city codes; if calling Shanghai or Beijing from abroad, drop the first zero.

People's Republic of China (☎86)

Shanghai (☎021)

Beijing (☎010)

Toilets

☑ **Top Tip** The golden rule is always to carry an emergency stash of toilet paper – you never know when you'll need it and many toilets are devoid of such essentials.

➡ Public toilets in Shanghai are numerous, but the quality of the experience varies greatly. In an emergency, look for a high-end hotel or a fast-food restaurant.

➡ Toilets in hotels are generally sitters, but expect to find squatters in many public toilets. In all but the cheapest hotels it's safe to flush toilet paper down the

toilet. If you see a small waste-paper basket in the corner of the toilet, that is where you should throw the toilet paper. Tampons always go in the basket.

➡ The Chinese characters for men and women are 男 (men) and 女 (women).

Tourist Information

☑ **Top Tip** Your hotel should be able to provide you with most of the tourist information you require. You can also pick up free maps of Shanghai and the metro at the airports.

Shanghai Call Centre

(☎962 288; ⏱24hr) This toll-free English-language hotline is possibly the most useful telephone number in Shanghai – it can even give your cab driver directions if you've got a mobile phone.

Shanghai Information Centre for International Visitors (☎6384 9366; No 2, Alley 123, Xingye Rd) Xintiandi information centre with currency exchange and free brochures.

Scams

'Hello, can you help us take photo?' This ostensibly harmless question is in fact one of the better hooks for Shanghai's main scam. Young people posing as students work the main tourist drags – the Bund, E Nanjing Rd and the exit of the Shanghai Museum – engaging tourists in conversation. However the conversation begins, it will inevitably end with an invitation to a 'traditional tea ceremony'. Intrigued? Don't be. You'll wind up with a US$100 bill and a private escort to the closest ATM.

Tourist Information & Service Centres (旅游咨询服务中心**)**

The standard of English varies from good to nonexistent, though most branches have free maps. Locations include the following:

The Bund Beneath the Bund promenade, opposite the intersection with E Nanjing Rd.

East Nanjing Road (518 Jiujiang Rd; 九江路518号)

Jing'an (Lane 1678, 19 W Nanjing Rd; 南京西路1678弄19号)

Yuyuan Gardens (149 Jiujiaochang Rd; 旧校场路149号)

Travellers with Disabilities

Shanghai's traffic, the city's frequent over- and underpasses and widespread indifference to the plight of the wheelchair-bound are the greatest challenges to travellers with disabilities. There may be 500,000 wheelchair users in the city, but metro system escalators don't go both ways.

An increasing number of modern buildings,

museums, stadiums and most new hotels are wheelchair accessible.

Visas

☑ **Top Tip** Start your visa paperwork about a month before your trip.

A visa is required for all visitors to China except for citizens of Japan, Singapore and Brunei. Visas can be obtained from Chinese embassies and consulates. Most tourists get a single-entry visa for

a 30-day stay, valid for three months from the date of issue. Longer-stay multiple-entry visas also exist, though obtaining one can be more of a hassle – it all depends upon the current rules at your local embassy.

Your passport must be valid for at least six months after the expiry date of your visa; at least one entire blank page in your passport is required for the visa.

Shanghai Dos & Don'ts

➡ When presenting your business card, proffer it with the first finger and thumb of both hands (thumbs on top).

➡ Don't stick your chopsticks vertically into your rice, but lay them down on your plate or on the chopstick rest.

➡ Always hand your cigarettes around in social situations.

➡ Don't insist on paying the dinner or bar bill if your fellow diner appears determined.

➡ Always offer to take your shoes off when entering a Chinese person's home.

➡ Biting your fingernails is a no-no.

➡ Losing face is about making people look stupid or forcing them to back down in front of others. Take care to avoid it and don't lose sight of your own face in the process.

Language

Mandarin Chinese – or Pǔtōnghuà (common speech), as it's referred to by the Chinese – can be written using the Roman alphabet. This system is known as Pinyin; in the following phrases we have provided both Mandarin script and Pinyin.

Mandarin has 'tonal' quality – the raising and lowering of pitch on certain syllables. There are four tones in Mandarin, plus a fifth 'neutral' tone that you can all but ignore. In Pinyin the tones are indicated with accent marks on vowels: **ā** (high), **á** (rising), **ǎ** (falling-rising), **à** (falling).

To enhance your trip with a phrase-book, visit **lonelyplanet.com**. Lonely Planet iPhone phrasebooks are available through the Apple App store.

Basics

Hello.	你好。	Nǐhǎo.
Goodbye.	再见。	Zàijiàn.
How are you?	你好吗?	Nǐhǎo ma?
Fine.	好。	Hǎo.
And you?	你呢?	Nǐ ne?
Please ...	请……	Qǐng ...
Thank you.	谢谢你。	Xièxie nǐ.
Excuse me.	劳驾。	Láojià.
Sorry.	对不起。	Duìbùqǐ.
Yes.	是。	Shì.
No.	不是。	Bùshì.

Do you speak English?

你会说	Nǐ huìshuō
英文吗?	Yīngwén ma?

I don't understand.

我不明白。	Wǒ bù míngbái.

Eating & Drinking

I'd like ...

我要……	Wǒ yào ...	
a table for two	一张两个人的桌子	yīzhāng liǎngge rén de zhuōzi
the drink list	酒水单	jiǔshuǐ dān
the menu	菜单	càidān
beer	啤酒	píjiǔ
coffee	咖啡	kāfēi

I don't eat ...

我不吃……	Wǒ bùchī ...	
fish	鱼	yú
poultry	家禽	jiāqín
red meat	牛羊肉	niúyángròu

Cheers!

干杯!	Gānbēi!

That was delicious.

真好吃。	Zhēn hǎochī.

The bill, please!

买单!	Mǎidān!

Shopping

I'd like to buy ...

我想买……	Wǒ xiǎng mǎi ...

I'm just looking.

我先看看。	Wǒ xiān kànkan.

How much is it?
多少钱？　　　Duōshǎo qián?

That's too expensive.
太贵了。　　　Tàiguì le.

Can you lower the price?
能便宜　　　Néng piányi
一点吗？　　yīdiǎn ma?

Emergencies

Help!　　救命！　Jiùmìng!
Go away!　走开！　Zǒukāi!

Call a doctor!
请叫医生来！　Qǐng jiào yīshēng lái!

Call the police!
请叫警察！　　Qǐng jiào jǐngchá!

I'm lost.
我迷路了。　　Wǒ mílù le.

I'm sick.
我生病了。　　Wǒ shēngbìng le.

Where are the toilets?
厕所在哪儿？　Cèsuǒ zài nǎr?

Time & Numbers

What time is it?
现在几点钟？　Xiànzài jǐdiǎn zhōng?

It's (10) o'clock.
(十)点钟。　　(Shí)diǎn zhōng.

Half past (10).
(十)点三十分。　(Shí)diǎn sānshífēn.

morning	早上	zǎoshang
afternoon	下午	xiàwǔ
evening	晚上	wǎnshàng
yesterday	昨天	zuótiān
today	今天	jīntiān
tomorrow	明天	míngtiān

1	一	yī
2	二/两	èr/liǎng
3	三	sān
4	四	sì
5	五	wǔ
6	六	liù
7	七	qī
8	八	bā
9	九	jiǔ
10	十	shí

Transport & Directions

Where's ...?
……在哪儿？　… zài nǎr?

What's the address?
地址在哪儿？　Dìzhǐ zài nǎr?

How do I get there?
怎么走？　　　Zěnme zǒu?

How far is it?
有多远？　　　Yǒu duō yuǎn?

Can you show me on the map?
请帮我找　　Qǐng bāngwǒ zhǎo
它在地图上　tā zài dìtú shàng
的位置。　　de wèizhi.

When's the next bus?
下一趟车　　Xià yītàng chē
几点走？　　jǐdiǎn zǒu?

A ticket to ...
一张到　　　Yīzhāng dào
……的票。　　… de piào.

Does it stop at ...?
在……能下　　Zài … néng xià
车吗？　　　chē ma?

I want to get off here.
我想这儿下车。　Wǒ xiǎng zhèr xiàchē.

Index

See also separate subindexes for:

🚫 **Eating p144**

🅟 **Drinking p145**

🅔 **Entertainment p145**

🅢 **Shopping p145**

Sights p000
Map Pages **p000**

Behind the Scenes

Send Us Your Feedback

We love to hear from travellers – your comments help make our books better. We read every word, and we guarantee that your feedback goes straight to the authors. Visit **lonelyplanet.com/contact** to submit your updates and suggestions.

Note: We may edit, reproduce and incorporate your comments in Lonely Planet products such as guidebooks, websites and digital products, so let us know if you don't want your comments reproduced or your name acknowledged. For a copy of our privacy policy visit lonelyplanet.com/privacy.

Our Readers

Many thanks to the travellers who used the last edition and wrote to us with helpful hints, useful advice and interesting anecdotes:

Alexander Dilg, Zhang Fan, Deidre Giacomin, Lara Müller, Adam Rudginsky

Christopher's Thanks

Much gratitude is due to Gerald and May Neumann for their hospitality

and great suggestions. Thanks as well to Miranda Yao, Wang Xinhai, Laure Romeyer, Sandy Chu, Lynn Ye, Caroline and Antoine Lebouc, Sam Maurey, Claudio Valsecchi and Munson Wu. Finally, special thanks to *Shanghai* co-author Damian Harper.

Acknowledgments

Cover photograph: Yuyuan Gardens, Shanghai, Yang Liu/Corbis

This Book

This 3rd edition of Lonely Planet's *Pocket Shanghai* guidebook was researched and written by Christopher Pitts. The previous edition was also written by Christopher Pitts. Damian Harper wrote the 1st edition.

Commissioning Editors Emily K Wolman, Kathleen Munnelly **Coordinating**

Editors Sarah Bailey, Carolyn Boicos **Coordinating Cartographer** Mark Griffiths **Coordinating Layout Designer** Lauren Egan **Managing Editors** Barbara Delissen, Martine Power **Senior Editors** Andi Jones, Catherine Naghten **Managing Cartographers** Corey Hutchison, Alison Lyall **Managing Layout Designer** Chris Girdler **Assisting**

Cartographer Jolyon Philcox **Cover Research** Naomi Parker **Internal Image Research** Nicholas Colicchia, Kylie McLaughlin **Language Content** Branislava Vladisavljevic

Thanks to Carolyn Bain, Sasha Baskett, Ryan Evans, Larissa Frost, Trent Paton, Raphael Richards, Phillip Tang, Diana Von Holdt, Gerard Walker

Our Writer

Christopher Pitts

Chris started off his university years studying classical Chinese poetry before a week in 1990s Shanghai (en route to school in Kunming) abruptly changed his focus to the idiosyncrasies of modern China. Several years in Asia memorising Chinese characters got him hooked, and he returns regularly to immerse himself in what is one of the world's most fascinating languages. A freelance writer, editor and translator, he's written for Lonely Planet's *Shanghai* since 2005 and Lonely Planet's *China* since 2004. Visit him online at www.christopherpitts.net.

Published by Lonely Planet Publications Pty Ltd
ABN 36 005 607 983
3rd edition – Apr 2013
ISBN 978 1 74179 963 7
© Lonely Planet 2013   Photographs © as indicated 2013
10 9 8 7 6 5 4 3 2 1
Printed in China